John Wrightson

Live stock

John Wrightson

Live stock

ISBN/EAN: 9783337124052

Printed in Europe, USA, Canada, Australia, Japan

Cover: Foto ©Suzi / pixelio.de

More available books at **www.hansebooks.com**

CASSELL'S AGRICULTURAL TEXT-BOOKS
(THE "DOWNTON" SERIES)

LIVE STOCK

BY

JOHN WRIGHTSON M.R.A.C. F.C.S.

PROFESSOR OF AGRICULTURE IN THE ROYAL COLLEGE OF SCIENCE SOUTH KENSINGTON
PRESIDENT OF THE COLLEGE OF AGRICULTURE DOWNTON SALISBURY
EXAMINER IN AGRICULTURE UNDER THE SCIENCE AND
ART DEPARTMENT ETC.

SECOND THOUSAND

CASSELL AND COMPANY LIMITED
LONDON PARIS & MELBOURNE
1893
ALL RIGHTS RESERVED

PREFACE.

In submitting this, the third book of the Agricultural Series, to the public, the authors believe that the information already given in the two previous volumes is most fittingly completed by a short treatise on Live Stock. The three natural divisions of agriculture are soils, crops, and live stock, and each of these sections has now been treated of in a manner which it is hoped will prove attractive and suggestive. It is impossible to entirely avoid adverse criticism. Books such as this are sometimes said to be too sketchy and diffuse, and sometimes too elaborate. An effort has been made to avoid both these faults, and to produce a work of real value to those who in after-life will be occupied in agricultural pursuits.

There are points of truly educational value in the study of live stock. There is, for example, the lesson of perseverance and ability abundantly evident in the efforts of the earlier improvers of our domestic animals. There is also the record of a great movement of national importance in the improvement of so many breeds of stock during the last hundred and fifty years. The diversity of breeds, and their adaptability to different soils and climates, or to different purposes, is also highly interesting and instructive, showing that no breed can be spoken of as the best, but that each is suited for its own particular surroundings.

The relations of our domesticated animals to wild forms from which they were derived, or to allied forms which still roam unrestrained over grassy plains, or wander through the trackless forest, is well worthy of attention. This aspect of our live stock has been carefully studied by many of our best naturalists, and it is hoped that the attention bestowed upon it in the following pages may stimulate a love of natural history, and throw an additional interest around such familiar forms as horses and cattle. Thus, at the very outset the question is asked, "Where do all these breeds of cattle, sheep, pigs, and horses come from?" and an effort has been made throughout the book to answer this interesting inquiry. The peculiarities of each breed are also given in clear language, and the relative merits of each are briefly discussed as an introduction to wider knowledge.

Live stock management may be treated of under the heads of origin, varieties, principles of breeding, methods of rearing and feeding, general management, and treatment during disease. All of these topics deserve study; but it is evident that the minuter treatment of animals suffering from disease must be left to the veterinary surgeon. On the other hand, the best methods of maintaining animals in a state of health, and of promoting rapid growth, are more properly the objects of the agriculturist, and these subjects are consequently more prominently put forward.

These Text Books are intended principally for those who require elementary instruction, but there are many points treated of which are worthy of the serious attention of practical farmers. The writer has in some measure advanced his treatment of the subject in the later pages of the present volume, feeling that the student who has carefully read the books treating of soils and manures, and of crops, may now be expected to take an interest in problems which might at the outset be beyond him. The chapter upon the horse which concludes the present Reader is written in a manner more suited to older students than some of the earlier chapters, or than the two previous Readers. This, it is submitted, is only natural in a work such as the present, in which a very considerable course of study, extending through three closely related books, is attempted. Although separate, the three volumes ought undoubtedly to be read consecutively, and to be considered as forming an elementary course of agricultural teaching.

Lastly, I must impress upon all students of agriculture, whether old or young, the vast importance of practical knowledge of animals, gained by looking after them. The directions given to pig-feeders lose half their meaning to anyone who has no pig to practise upon. The same is true of every kind of stock, and it is the actual contact, the actual exchange of opinions, coupled with reading, which, taken together, form the basis of practical knowledge.

It has been objected that books of this description are calculated to turn out men who are wanting in substantial practical knowledge. If the whole of a man's knowledge of farming is gathered from books, such an accusation would be true. As, however, the writer has been himself actively engaged in farming for a number of years, he is fully alive to the necessity of practical knowledge, and it is his firm conviction that knowledge gained by reading and hearing can only be reduced to practice by actual performance. Agricultural knowledge is not a natural instinct, but must be communicable, whether from father to son, or teacher to pupil; and it must be an extraordinary pursuit, indeed, if its principles and its operations cannot, to some extent, be reduced to writing! Of this, however, there can be no doubt. The only caution which it is necessary to impress upon all students is that theory must go hand in hand with practice. This statement may even be pushed farther. It is not too much to say that while many successful farmers have not studied the theory of their business in books, and are therefore purely practical men, it is impossible to find a successful farmer who owes all his knowledge to books. Still, it does not follow that the study of agriculture is useless. On the contrary, the best agriculturists have always been found among men whose ears are open to every suggestion and to the teachings of science.

JOHN WRIGHTSON.

COLLEGE OF AGRICULTURE, DOWNTON.
February, 1892.

CONTENTS.

CHAPTER I.
BRITISH RACES OF CATTLE.

	PAGE
Cattle	1
Origin of our Domestic Animals	2
Chillingham Cattle	3
Our Breeds of Cattle—	7
1. Shorthorn Cattle	7
2. Hereford Cattle	11
3. Devon Cattle	13
4. Sussex Cattle	14
5. Norfolk Red-Polled	16
6. Longhorns	18
7. Welsh (Pembroke) Cattle	19
8. Black Galloways	20
9. The Kerry Cow	21
10. The Polled Aberdeenshire and Angus Breeds	21
11. The West Highland Breed	23
12. The Ayrshire Breed	24
13. The Jersey Breed	24
14. The Guernsey Breed	26

CHAPTER II.
MANAGEMENT OF CATTLE.

Cows and Calves	30
The Calf	33
Veal Calves	33
Bull Calves	34

	PAGE
Ordinary Weanling Calves	34
Calves during their First Summer	37
Calves during their Second Winter	37
Management of Yearlings and Two-year-olds	37
Fattening of Cattle	38
Practice of Fattening Cattle	44
Profits from Fattening Cattle	47

CHAPTER III.

DAIRY MANAGEMENT.

Management of Milking Cows in Winter	49
Preparation of the Food	51
Effect of Food on Milk	52
Milk easily affected by its Surroundings	53
Separating Cream from Milk	54
The Laval Separator	58
Butter-making	61
The Dairy	62
Ripening of Cream	63
Churning	64
Cheese-making	72
Cheddar Cheese-making	73
Concluding Remarks	79

CHAPTER IV.

SHEEP.

Relation of Sheep and Cattle to Wild Animals	81
British Sheep	82
Long-woolled Sheep	83
Short-woolled Sheep	84
Forest and Mountain Breeds	84
Principal Breeds	85

CONTENTS. xiii

PAGE

Long-woolled Sheep—
    1. The Leicester Breed 85
    2. The Border Leicester 86
    3. The Wensleydale Breed 86
    4. The Lincoln Breed 87
    5. Devon Longwools 87
    6. Romney Marsh Breed 88
    7. The Cotswold Race 89

Short-woolled Sheep—
    8. Southdown 89
    9. The Hampshire Down Breed 92
    10. The Suffolk Down 94
    11. The Shropshire Sheep 94
    12. The Oxford Down 96
    13. The Dorset Horn Sheep 97

Mountain and Forest Breeds—
    14. The Heath, or Black-faced Breed 97
    15. The Cheviot Breed 99
    16. The Herdwick Race 99
    17. The Lonk Breed 100
    18. The Crag Sheep 100
    19. The Exmoor Breed 101
    20. The Dartmoor Breed 101
    21. The Roscommon Breed 101
    22. The Ryland Breed 102

CHAPTER V.

MANAGEMENT OF SHEEP.

Sheep Breeding 104
Different Systems of Breeding Sheep—Ram Breeding 104
Breeding Fat Lambs 105
Breeding Store Lambs 105
Management of Ewes 106

	PAGE
General Treatment	108
A young Ewe Flock	109
The Lambing Season	110
Young Lambs (January Lambing)	113
Young Lambs (March Lambing)	115
Hill Lambs	116
Fattening Sheep	117
Great Economy of Sheep Folding	118
Turnips for Sheep	119
The Food of Fattening Sheep	121
Practical Directions for the Fattening of Sheep	122
Method of Feeding	124
Cutting Turnips	124

CHAPTER VI.

VARIOUS EVENTS IN THE LIFE OF A SHEEP.

Birth	126
Castration	126
Tailing	127
Weaning	127
Washing	128
Dipping	129
Shearing	130
Flies and Foot-rot	133
Liver-rot	136
Scab	138

CHAPTER VII.

PIGS.

Origin of the Pig	141
The Wild Boar	142
Chinese Pig	145
South European Pigs	146

CONTENTS.

English Breeds of Pigs—
  The Black Breeds—
    1. The Berkshire Breed ... 146
    2. The Essex Race ... 147
    3. Other Black Races ... 148
    4. The Tamworth Race ... 148
  The White Breeds—
    5. Large and Small Yorkshires ... 149
    6. Other White Breeds ... 150

CHAPTER VIII.
MANAGEMENT OF PIGS.

The Breeding of Pigs ... 151
Sows ... 153
Farrowing ... 154
Store Pigs ... 155
Fatting Pigs ... 156
Bacon Curing ... 159
Wiltshire Bacon ... 162
Curing Hams ... 163
Sweet Hams ... 163

CHAPTER IX.
HORSES.

The Origin of the Horse ... 165
The African Horse ... 167
The Asiatic Horse ... 168
The Arabian Horse ... 168
The Wild Horses of South America ... 169
Darwin's Views as to the Origin of the Horse ... 170
English Horses ... 171
English Cart-horses ... 174
The Old English Black Horse ... 176

The Clydesdale Horse	178
The Suffolk Punch	180
The Cleveland Bay	180
The Hackney Horse	181
Ponies and Galloways	182
Asses and Mules	184

CHAPTER X.

MANAGEMENT OF HORSES.

Breeding Horses	189
Treatment of Weanling Colts	191
Treatment of Yearling Colts	191
Treatment of Two-year-old Colts	192
Breaking-in Cart Colts	192
Management of Working Horses	193
Feeding of Farm Horses	195

LIVE STOCK.

CHAPTER I.

BRITISH RACES OF CATTLE.

GREAT BRITAIN is rich in breeds of live stock of all kinds. Why this should be so is not easy to explain but it has been the case for many hundreds of years. The Venerable Bede, who wrote almost twelve hundred years ago, says: "Britain excels for grain and trees, and is well adapted for feeding cattle and beasts of burden. The climate of Great Britain is suited for cattle and sheep as the summers are comparatively cool and moist, and the winters are mild. The growth of grass is abundant, and the mountains, hills, and vales favour the breeding of different races, suitable for each situation.

We shall find no difficulty in describing fourteen breeds of cattle and twenty breeds of sheep, including the cattle and sheep of Ireland, all comprised in a comparatively small area, and each owned by breeders who take the greatest possible pains in improving them.

CATTLE.

Neat cattle, or bullocks, naturally come first in describing our races of live stock. One of the first questions which would occur to any person who notices the many sorts of cattle, say at a great agricultural show, would be—

Where do all these breeds come from? and how have they been brought to such perfection? It is the object of the following pages to answer this question, and in doing so we must go a long way back in the history of England, and touch upon that of other countries.

Origin of our Domestic Animals.

All of our domesticated animals, no doubt, at one time lived in the wild state. It is, however, a curious fact that there is no such thing as a truly wild horse, bullock, or sheep which may be said to be the form from which our domesticated horses, cattle, and sheep have sprung. This is not true of the pig, for we see in the wild boar of the forests of Germany an animal which can be readily domesticated, and which may soon be converted into a domestic pig. As we often hear of wild horses, it is well to state that they are not exactly wild animals in the sense that lions and tigers, antelopes and deer, are wild, but that they are the descendants of horses which were domesticated, but have escaped into the forests and prairies, and become wild. When America was first discovered by Columbus there were no horses to be seen, and the first were imported by the Spanish soldiers who went across the Atlantic Ocean to conquer the New World. It is from these that the wild horses of America are descended. In the same manner the wild horses of Tartary are considered to be escaped rather than wild, and no one knows what the original wild horse was like, except that he was probably, in many respects, like his domesticated descendants. A great deal has been written upon this subject, the general opinion being that the wild horse, before he was tamed, was a more or less striped animal, like a quagga or zebra, and probably cream-coloured between the stripes. You see, then, that the wild horse has so completely disappeared from the face of the earth that clever naturalists can only speculate or give their ideas as to what he was like.

The same general fact is also true of cattle, for, in spite of the great number of breeds, no one knows what the parent form was like; but it is thought that at least three different species were originally domesticated, all of which have ceased to live an entirely independent life. Bones of cattle have been discovered among the oldest remains of human habitations, and these have been carefully examined, with the result that they seem always to belong to one of these three species.

Chillingham Cattle.

The nearest approach to a wild ox in Great Britain is to be found in the Earl of Tankerville's park at Chillingham, in Northumberland. They are known as wild cattle, and have many of the instincts of wild animals. That they are not truly wild is shown by the fact that they are confined within a park, like the herds of fallow deer so often seen, and that they have, to a certain extent, to be looked after and fed in the winter. Still, they are fully as wild as pheasants, and, as the late Charles Darwin says, "in their habits and instincts are truly wild." Thus, the cows hide their calves in the bushes and long grass, and visit them from time to time to suckle them. The calves lie close, and crouch in their lair when any one approaches. The animals, when grown up, are very wary, and always fly when man attempts to intrude upon them. The herd gallops off along the bottoms of the valleys, and is difficult to find, because it generally succeeds in placing a hill between itself and its pursuer. The bulls form a ring around the cows and young calves in case of attack, and present a bold front to the enemy. All these habits are very unlike those of ordinary domesticated cattle, so that the Chillingham cattle may be said to be wild, although they are confined to a park. There are other herds of wild cattle besides those at Chillingham: as, for example, those of the Duke of Hamilton, and Lord Ferrers at Chartley, and at Burton Constable.

Fig. 1.—HEAD OF CHILLINGHAM BULL.

These cattle are considered to represent an otherwise extinct original race, known to naturalists as *Bos primigenius*. They are white, with black rims to the eyes, black muzzles, black hoofs, and black tips to the horns. The inside of the ears is reddish-brown, and the flanks and shoulders are shaded with grey.

Cattle of somewhat similar character are to be found in Hungary, on the banks of the Danube, and these, although domesticated and used for purposes of draught and for fatting, have still a good deal of wildness in their nature. They are not safe to approach on foot, and the cows hide their young ones among bushes and scrub. They are in colour very similar to the cattle of Chillingham, and are considered to be descendants of *Bos primigenius*. The cattle of Spain and of Italy are also similar to them.

Returning to Great Britain, we believe that the black cattle of Wales and the red cattle of Devonshire, and probably those of Sussex, are also descended from the same stock, although now bred of a different colour.

The remaining two forms* from which our cattle are descended are only to be found in the domesticated condition, so that the one trace we have of the truly wild cattle which at one time roamed over Britain is now to be found in a few ancient parks, where the animals are highly valued by their owners. The Highland cattle are probably descended from one extinct type (*longifrons*), and the other, if present at all, exists only in the form of crosses in modified descendants.

The differences of colour of our breeds of cattle are not difficult to account for, as domesticated animals tend to vary in colour. Wild animals always are the same, as a little observation will show. Wild rabbits, rats, mice, ferrets, cats, pigeons, and almost all other wild animals, are uniform in colour. But tame rabbits, rats, mice, ferrets, cats, pigeons, etc., are always of different colours. So it is with our larger domesticated animals. This appears to be

* These are known to naturalists as *Bos longifrons* and *Bos frontosus*.

a law of nature, for it is seen in plants as well as in animals. As soon as a plant is cultivated it begins to throw sports or varieties, and the gardener soon obtains a large number of different sorts.

Not only do domesticated animals and cultivated plants differ from the original form in colour, but also in size and in other peculiarities, and hence we see in the mere fact of domestication a reason why there are so many varieties of cattle, sheep, and other sorts of live stock in the country. Animals are also bred according to certain "fancies" of the breeder. In one country black may be the favourite colour, and in another red or grey, and hence breeds become established through the course of years.

Soil, climate, and food also produce their effects. On small islands like the Shetlands or Orkneys both horses and cattle become small, and on exposed situations or on mountains, small cattle and horses, like the Kerry cows or the Exmoor ponies, are to be seen. It is curious to notice how quickly sheep of a certain breed alter in character when removed to a new soil and climate; and the same is true of cattle.

We see, then, the explanation of our many races of cattle: first in the fact that they are descended from at least three original types or species of ox; second, in the law which appears to encourage differences of form and colour whenever animals are domesticated; third, in the fancies of breeders who try to breed their animals according to their ideas of what constitutes a good type; fourth, to the gradual changes brought about by different soils, climates, and food.

Lastly, and added to the above, we have another cause

in the crossing of races so as to produce new forms. Many of our best breeds of live stock have been produced by crossing two or more breeds together. The English race-horse was produced by crossing high-class English horses with Arab, Turcoman, and Barb blood. The Clydesdale horse was produced by crossing Scotch horses with those imported from Flanders. The Shorthorn is no doubt a crossed race, and we should probably find that nearly all our races of cattle and sheep have been crossed at some time. As for pigs, they owe their properties in a great measure to crossing with Chinese and Italian pigs.

OUR BREEDS OF CATTLE.

Having done something to clear the mind of the reader as to why we have so many different descriptions of cattle, we will, in the next place, pass the principal races in review, and in tracing their history we shall meet with fresh cases, showing the effects of the general laws which have been already, to some extent, explained.

1. Shorthorn Cattle.

No kind of cattle is more highly thought of than the Shorthorn. They are now found in every county of England, Scotland, and Ireland, unless in purely mountainous parts, where hardier races are preferred. Everyone knows the Shorthorn by sight. Whenever we see a drove of cattle of mixed colour, varying from red to white or mixed red and white, we are probably looking at Shorthorns. On closer inspection we notice that they are square in outline, mossy in coat, cream-coloured around the eye and muzzle, and of moderate length in the horns. These are, no doubt, Shorthorns. They may not be quite purely bred or of the best quality, but the general features just mentioned declare them to belong to this

Fig. 2.—SHORTHORN COW, "DARLINGTON 15TH."

race. So generally distributed are they that many persons might say that they thought all cattle were about the same as have been described.

Shorthorns are a North Country breed, their first home having been in Yorkshire and Durham. They were there for a long time before they spread over the rest of the country, and were first improved by two brothers, Robert

Fig. 3.—THE MARQUIS OF EXETER'S SHORTHORN FAMILY AT THE ROYAL.
1, Sea Bird; 2, Sea Lark; 3, Telemachus 9th; 4, Sea Gull; 5, Telemachus 6th.

and Charles Colling, of Brampton and Ketton, in the county of Durham. The brothers Colling, and especially Charles, appear to have had a great natural taste for the improvement of stock. They learnt a great deal from Mr. Bakewell, of Dishley, in Leicestershire, who ought to be mentioned, because before his time no one seems to have thought much about this important subject. Bakewell undertook the improvement of horses, sheep, and cattle, and produced the improved English black horse, the Leicester sheep, and Longhorn cattle. Charles Colling used to stay at Dishley, and determined to improve the cattle of his own neighbourhood. The name Shorthorn was most likely adopted as a sort of contrast to Bakewell's Longhorn, and the rival race soon became the greater favourite. The brothers Colling were very successful, and their herds became the foundation of every other herd of Shorthorns in the country. Mr. Thomas Bates, of Kirklevington, and Mr. Booth, of Warlaby, were also engaged in the same pursuit during the life-time of the Collings. The great success of the Shorthorns as a breed appears to be due to its combining the properties of milking and beef-producing in a high degree, and also to the very early age at which they are ready for the butcher. Before the time of the brothers Colling cattle were seldom fattened till they were four years old, but, owing to the improvement caused by careful breeding, animals were produced fit for slaughter at two years old. The points arrived at by all the early and later breeders of these cattle have been early maturity, beauty of form, a reduced quantity of offal, and quick power of fattening or laying on flesh. Shorthorns, combined with these qualities great milking properties, and being also very attractive in appearance and exceedingly docile, it is no wonder that they should have quickly spread over the country, and even into foreign lands.

2. Hereford Cattle.

These cattle differ from Shorthorns both in colour and form. The Hereford may be described, indeed, as red and white, but the two colours are always seen in the same parts of the animal. A Hereford may be described as red, with white face, breast, belly, feet, top of tail, and over the tops of the shoulders. This gives a uniform appearance, which contrasts with the varied colours of the Shorthorn. In form, the Hereford is longer than the Shorthorn, its shoulders and fore-end are deeper, and its buttocks are not let down quite so straight. The late Mr. Dixon, who wrote upon cattle, tells us that the peculiar white face of the Hereford was not always a characteristic, but was introduced by the birth of a bull calf with a white face towards the close of the last century. This particular feature was admired, and became fashionable, and by the use of this animal as a sire the feature was propagated until the whole of the modern Herefords became red, with white faces. There are also light and dark-grey Hereford, with white faces, but all the animals one sees at shows are described as red with white faces. As a beef-producer the Hereford is probably equal to the Shorthorn, and the meat is of a more marbled appearance, owing to the fat and lean being better mixed. They, however, are inferior to Shorthorns as dairy cattle.

Fig. 4.—A. ROGERS' HEREFORD BULL, "GRATEFUL."

3. Devon Cattle.

The Devons are an exceedingly symmetrical and beautiful race of cattle, found in North and South Devonshire. They are rich red in colour, and are much smaller than either of the last two breeds. Like most small breeds,

Fig. 5.—MR. W. FARTHING'S DEVON COW, "PRETTY FACE."

they are beautifully formed, and excel in this particular either the Shorthorn or the Hereford. One remarkable feature in these cattle is the large size of the oxen, as compared with either bulls or cows. A Devon ox, indeed, grows to a very great size, and is one of the most useful cattle for draught which we possess in England. It is, of course, seldom that cattle are used for ploughing, but where the practice is still followed a pair of Devon steers will beat any other kind of oxen either for quickness of step, or for strength. Devon cattle are red all over, with the exception of an occasional patch of white upon, or just in front of, the udder. The skin around the eyes, inside the ears, and around the muzzle is of rich yellow or orange colour, and the base of the horn is sometimes of the same hue. This enlivens the features, and gives a certain brightness of colour to the face. The hair is sometimes smooth, and in other cases deep and curly, mossy, and the coat is mottled, or what is often called "hammer-marked." In form the Devon is particularly smooth on the shoulders, and well filled up behind them. Like the Hereford, the quarters are not quite straight, and the buttocks are somewhat rounded as compared with the square-made Shorthorn. They are excellent producers of beef, but not so much of milk. They are highly esteemed in their own county, as well as in Dorset, Somerset, Wiltshire, and Hampshire. A great many also find their way into graziers' hands in Norfolk and other eastern counties. The beef is of high quality, and is considered by some to be superior to that of any other breed. The milk, although less abundant, is richer than that produced by the Shorthorn.

4. Sussex Cattle.

No breed of cattle has made more progress of late years than the Sussex. They are red in colour, and are very similar to the Devons, but a slight examination will show them to be distinctly larger in size, looser in form,

Fig. 6.—E. AND A. STANFORD'S SUSSEX BULL.

and darker in complexion, swarthy or dark in feature, and the bright colours of the Devon are at once missed when the two are compared. The Sussex is one of the beef-producing races, and in this respect is fully equal to any other breed. The farmers of Sussex are proud of their cattle, and have of late years taken great pains to bring them to perfection.

5. Norfolk Red-Polled.

Of late years, and especially since the revival of interest in dairy-farming, the Norfolk red-polled cattle have been much talked of and written about. Upwards of a hundred years ago Suffolk, and to some extent Norfolk, were dairying counties; and the Suffolk polls or Suffolk dun cattle were considered to be famous milkers. There was, however, a long period during which corn-growing was more profitable than dairy-work, and, besides, it was less troublesome. Norfolk especially became almost entirely a corn-growing and grazing county, and the cares of the dairy were left to smaller men in other counties. The old Suffolk Dun was a yellow-red cow, supposed to have been descended from Galloway cattle, which had been brought in droves from Wigtonshire and Kirkcudbright, in the south-west of Scotland. These cows, crossed with the cattle of the district, gradually produced a milking animal known as the Suffolk poll; and the Norfolk red poll of the present day seems to have originated from them. The Norfolk red poll bears a great resemblance to the Sussex, but the horn is wanting, and in its place is the knot or high poll which always is seen in dodded or hornless cattle. The Norfolk red poll is well described by its name,

Davyson 3rd. Silent Lady. Dolly.
Fig. 7.—A GROUP OF RED-POLLED CATTLE.

as it is always of the same uniform rich red colour, and free from horns. The cows are deep milkers, and they are well adapted for yielding large quantities of milk for the supply of towns.

6. Longhorns.

The Longhorn appears to have originally belonged to the Craven Valley, lying in West Yorkshire and East

Fig. 8.—HEAD OF LONGHORN (HEREFORD).

Lancashire. Similar cattle are to be found in Anglesea. They are interesting as having been the first race which were improved by selection and careful breeding. Robert Bakewell, of Dishley, Loughborough, Leicestershire, was a breeder of stock about 1763, and for many years later, and one of his achievements was the bringing out of the Longhorns. As already mentioned, the Shorthorn followed; but we can never forget that Bakewell led the way, and that the improvement of every other race of cattle followed, owing to the great example and success of Bakewell. These cattle are very long in the horns, which grow downwards, and turn in at the points towards the cheek or jaw. They are often over thirty inches in length, and have been known to be forty-two inches long in the cow. In colour the Longhorn is brindled with mixed red, yellow, and black, and white or pied along the back and belly. The carcase is long, and the stature somewhat low. The breed is, therefore, very distinct in character, or unlike any other race. So successful was Bakewell in improving these cattle that they became very popular all over England, and Longhorn herds were found in almost every county. They, however, met with a successful rival in the Shorthorn, and the Longhorn is now only found in small numbers. The late Duke of Buckingham was a breeder of Longhorns, and some very excellent specimens of the breed were to be seen at the Windsor Show in 1889.

7. Welsh (Pembroke) Cattle.

These are best represented by the Pembrokes, a breed of black, light-fleshed cattle, occasionally varied with a little white. The correct colour is, however, black, with a little white about the region of the udder. The horns, hoofs, muzzle, and rims of the eyes are also black. These cattle are probably of ancient origin, and closely connected with the park cattle of Chillingham and *Bos Primigenius*.

They are scarcely equal to any of the breeds already mentioned for producing beef, but are a hardy and useful

Fig. 9.—MR. G. F. BOWDEN'S PEMBROKE BULL AND HEIFER.

race, both for the fatting stall and dairy. An improved black Welsh race is known as the **Castle Martins**.

8. Black Galloways.

North of the Solway Firth, and extending southward to the same latitude as Durham, there is a peninsula, including the counties of Wigton, Kirkcudbright, and Dumfries, inhabited by a distinct and interesting breed of cattle known as Galloways. They are jet-black and hornless, strongly built, and rather low of stature. These cattle are hardy in constitution, and are much esteemed as producers of beef. The Galloway cattle are rarely housed, and the calves are allowed to suck their dams. The profits of their owners are derived from the sale of young cattle to the English graziers in the northern counties, and as far south as Norfolk. The Galloway is generally considered to have been the foundation of the Suffolk dun, and, by many, of the Norfolk red-poll, which are now famous as milkers. Be this as it may, the Galloways are as a rule only poor dairy cattle, and the custom of allowing the calves to suck their dams is not likely to increase the milking properties of the race. We were, however, recently informed that many Galloway cows are equal to Ayrshires in the production of milk.

9. The Kerry Cow.

The Kerry breed is now a favourite one where one or two cows are kept for supplying a family with milk. They are very small, and entirely black. Their form is slender, and they are well adapted for being made pets of. In older books they are described as having a white ridge along the back, but the most approved type of animal is now entirely black, with the exception of a small patch of white just in front of the udder. Kerry cows are wonderful milkers for their size. They are to be seen in large numbers in the mountainous parts of Kerry. There is a short-legged and thicker type of Kerry, which has received the distinctive name of the **Dexter Breed**.

10. The Polled Aberdeenshire and Angus Breeds.

These breeds have often been separately described. Both are polled and black, and inhabit the north-eastern

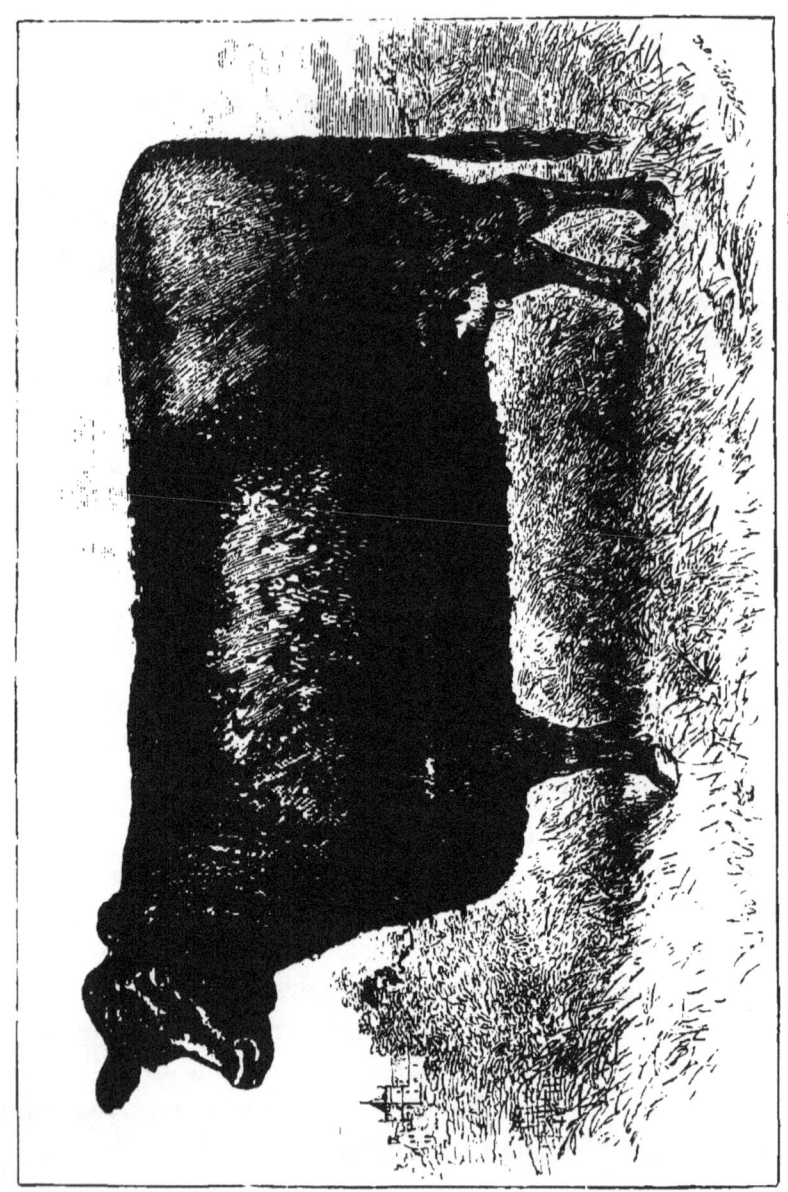

Fig. 10.—THE DUKE OF FIFE'S ABERDEEN BLACK-POLLED COW, "INNES."

BRITISH RACES OF CATTLE.

peninsula of which Aberdeenshire forms a part. They may be considered practically as one breed, and may be said to bear a general resemblance to the Galloway cattle, but are longer in the limb and looser in build. They are now described as the Aberdeen-Angus breed. They form a striking class at the annual show at Islington Hall, and are peculiar for their level carcases, length of body, total blackness of colour, and massive and hornless heads. The cows are better milkers than the Galloways.

11. The West Highland Breed.

This is a hardy race which inhabits the western and

Fig. 11.—WEST HIGHLAND COW.

central Highlands, and is found in great perfection in Argyleshire and the neighbouring western islands. They are exceedingly symmetrical in form, and their long, upright horns, shaggy coats, varied colour, and bold mien render them ornamental and picturesque. A fine herd which the author recently saw in Windsor Park possessed all these features in a marked degree. They were yellowish-brown, black, silver-grey, or brindled in colour, and their fine carriage rivalled that of the red deer, or the wild cattle of Chillingham. The West Highland cattle are beef-producers rather than dairy cattle, and yield meat of the highest quality. They are often to be seen grazing in the marshes of Norfolk and other famous grazing districts, from whence they find their way to the London cattle markets.

12. The Ayrshire Breed.

In the Ayrshire breed we find one of the best of our dairy races. They are red and white or yellow and white, and occasionally self-coloured, and shaded to dark browns. They are of medium size, are very hardy, and yield a large quantity of milk, well adapted for cheese-making. The Ayrshire cow will thrive upon land of comparatively poor character, and a larger number of them can be kept than of Shorthorns. The Ayrshire cow is the very type of a milking animal, being long and narrow in the head, angular in form, thin of flesh, and is deservedly popular.

13. The Jersey Breed.

No cow is more generally known than the Jersey. She is a great favourite with householders who keep a cow or two for their private use. Jersey cattle are exceedingly pretty, and are peculiar for a deer-like head, large, soft, prominent eyes, curved horns, and are of medium size. The skin is yellow, and the hair is shaded from a light fawn to dark

Fig. 12.—DUKE OF BUCCLEUCH'S AYRSHIRE COW, "LADY KILBURNE."

grey. The general tint is well described as smoke-coloured, and approaches that of many of the mountain races of Switzerland and the Tyrol. The value of the Jersey consists rather in the richness than the quantity of her milk; she is essentially a butter cow. Both her milk and butter are of rich colour, and a small number are often kept in large dairies for the purpose of imparting a richer appearance to the milk and butter. This is not a beef-producing breed, as they lay on flesh slowly, and the steers are difficult to fatten.

14. The Guernsey Breed.

This is another of the Channel Island races. It differs from the Jersey in being patchy yellow and white in colour, and in being somewhat ampler in form. It is a capital and rich milker and good butter cow, and is also kept largely by private householders in the neighbourhood of towns. We have now named and described the principal races of cattle found in the British Isles. They will be seen to be easily divisible into beef-producing and dairy cattle, while some, but especially the Shorthorn, are equally useful for both purposes. The best beef-producing breeds are the Shorthorns, Hereford, Sussex, Devon, Galloway, Aberdeen-Angus, and West Highlanders; while the most famous milk-producers are the Shorthorns, Ayrshire, Jersey, Guernsey, Norfolk Red-Polls, and Kerrys.

Fig. 13.—CHANNEL ISLAND CATTLE.

1, Mr. Le Brun's Jersey bull, "Duke;" 2, Mr. J. Watson's Jersey cow, "Florence;" 3, Mr. S. Barker Booth's Jersey heifer, "Favourite."

CHAPTER II.

MANAGEMENT OF CATTLE.

THE management of cattle naturally divides itself into their breeding, rearing, and fattening, the management of dairy cows, and the treatment of animals during illness. It will be easily seen that a great deal might be written upon each of these subjects. The breeding of cattle is a most important part of pastoral and arable farming, and where high-bred or pedigree stocks are kept a vast deal of knowledge is required, as well as a great amount of money. A single cow has been known to realise £2,000, and hundreds are often expended upon the purchase of one individual. In ordinary cases the breeding and rearing of calves entails a large amount of attention, and various methods are adopted, so that in all cases the breeding of cattle is a subject to which a book might well be devoted. Still, it is possible to give the principal facts in such a manner as to convey a fair idea as to what farmers ought to know. Many persons who bring up cattle from their birth have read very little about them; in such cases experience takes the place of book-knowledge, and even those who have learnt their business entirely by practising it may still learn a good deal from books. The fattening of cattle is an art which has lately been much improved by a study of the chemistry of foods, and of the organs of digestion and assimilation, or the wonderful power possessed by animals of changing grass, straw, turnips, and other foods, into beef, milk, and other products.

The management of dairy cows, and the best means of converting their milk into butter and cheese, has received a great deal of attention, and thick volumes have appeared upon this important subject. Perhaps no part of agricultural occupation has been more improved during the last twenty years, and those who wish to know all about it must travel far beyond the pages of this little book. Similarly, veterinary surgeons have expended an immense amount of labour in describing the diseases to which cattle are liable, and the best treatment of animals or herds when affected with disease. Some of these diseases may be communicated to people who eat the flesh or consume the milk of diseased cattle. Others are highly contagious or infectious, while others again appear in particular conditions favourable for their development, and become the cause of heavy losses. Take, for example, the cattle plague which visited our shores in 1864-5. This dreadful disease destroyed millions of cattle, and in many cases swept off entire herds. The history of these visitations, and the best means of checking them, have exercised the minds of the most able men, and are well worthy of consideration.

It is well to reflect for a moment upon the extent of knowledge required before a person can really understand all about cattle; and this should be a check upon the conceit which often accompanies ignorance. A good cattle man may understand enough to milk a cow, churn the butter, or make a good cheese, but in these days a more varied knowledge is highly desirable, and it is the object of these pages to at least show the nature of such knowledge, and to encourage deeper study.

Cows and Calves.

Cows are valuable as producers of milk and calves. No matter how high-priced a cow may be, the objects for which she is kept and tended are undoubtedly her milk and her progeny. The high value attached to certain cows is due to the consideration that they are able to transmit their good qualities to their offspring, whether male or female, and this constitutes the value of well-bred or pedigree stock. We should, however, never forget that a cow which will not milk or produce beef is useless, and ought not to be kept. The best cow is the animal which produces the best and largest quantity of milk, and of calves that may be turned into beef or into profitable cows.

The slight sketch of the various breeds of cattle just given shows that some races are peculiarly milkers, while others are beef-producers, and it would be foolish to expect a quick result in fattening from a Jersey, or an immense flow of milk from a Galloway cow. The peculiar properties of each breed must be kept in mind, but usefulness in one form or another is necessary.

Cows generally calve in the spring, a short time before the grass begins to grow, and they continue to yield a large quantity of milk throughout the summer. This is the most profitable way of keeping cows, because no kind of food is so good or so cheap as grass. If cows drop their calves in autumn they give milk during the winter, but it is never so abundant, and the food upon which the cow is fed is much more expensive. It is, therefore, clear that the best time for cows to calve is the early spring. As there is no rule without an exception, we may add that milk must be produced in winter as well as in summer, and that, therefore, some cows must calve in the autumn. It is necessary to pay the farmer more for milk produced in the winter than in the summer, because it is produced at a greater cost, and this induces some farmers to keep up their supply of milk both winter and summer. It is generally allowed that it is most profitable to produce milk when the grass is growing. In cheese-making districts the same rule holds good, and the cows are timed to calve in February, March, and April, so as to be in "full profit" during the grazing season. By November the cows are allowed to dry off, and their new season commences after again calving in the early spring. When cows are dry they will live very well upon straw and a few turnips, and hence the cost of food during the entire year is reduced to a *minimum*, while upon grass the yield of milk is kept at the *maximum*.

One acre of grass, rented at £3, will keep a cow from April 15th to September 30th, or for twenty-four weeks, at a cost (for food) of 2s. 6d. per week. During October she will receive hay, and gradually stop milking. In November, December, and January she will be in straw-yard, at a cost (in food) of about 2s. per week. After calving, and until there is a good bit of grass, she will again receive hay, and the entire cost of food will average about 3s. per week throughout the year. This is at once a cheap and economical way of keeping cows.

Well-managed cows produce a calf every year, and yield milk for nine or ten months. The amount of milk given by a good cow ranges from 600 to possibly 1,000 gallons over the whole period, and in some cases even larger quantities have been given. A cow that has newly calved may yield as much as seven gallons every day, but in ordinary cases four or five gallons are considered good. The amount given per day gradually diminishes as the cow becomes old in milk and heavy in calf, and at from two to three months before calving she is dried off.

Cows should always be gently used, and carefully milked and tended. It is of great importance to milk them thoroughly, as imperfect milking is sure to be followed by a lessened flow of milk. Well-bred or pedigree cows ought not to require more attention than ordinary cattle under good management should receive, and it is a mistake to imagine that high-bred cows are delicate. Cows should be driven to and from their pastures slowly, and should not be hurried through doors or gateways, but allowed plenty of time, to avoid pushing or crowding. Cows are sensitive creatures, and are easily frightened. They are also soon aware of kindness and gentle usage, and repay their attendants by yielding more milk. If a cow is roughly used, she is able to hold back her milk. When cows are timed to calve in the spring the feeding is a very simple affair, as it consists in turning them out to graze, but when milk is desired in winter the feeding is much more complicated and expensive.

As cows approach the period of calving they are dried off and turned into straw-yards, and receive a few roots or water, and in some instances 2 or 3 lbs. of oil-cake. Cows ought to be kept in fair condition, and should not be allowed to become fat, nor yet to become weak or low. They usually calve without assistance, but a good dairyman should watch over cows before and after the time of calving, and be ready to assist both the dam and her calf. It is seldom necessary to call in the assistance of a veterinary surgeon.

The Calf.

As soon as a calf is born it requires attention. There are two methods of dealing with calves. The first is the natural method of leaving it to its mother, who fondles and licks it dry, and encourages it to rise on to its feet and suck. When a calf is on its legs and finds the teat, immediate anxiety is over, and probably all will go well. It is a good plan to give a cow a comforting and laxative drench or drink both before and after calving. The simplest drink is $\frac{1}{2}$ lb. of Epsom salts, given either in warm water or beer, and a tablespoonful of ground ginger. There are also good drenches sold by druggists for this purpose. The second method of dealing with young calves is to take them from their dams as soon as they are dropped, and to rub them dry with wisps of straw. The cow is then milked, and the calf is fed with about a pint of the first milk, which is different to the milk yielded later. In all cases it is necessary to milk a cow immediately after she has calved. When the calf is allowed to suck its dam it does so after she has been milked, sufficient being left in the udder for the calf. Veal calves require a full supply of milk, but calves intended for weaning may be kept a little less liberally.

Veal Calves

should be allowed as much new milk as they can take; should be tied up, and not allowed any exercise, and be kept in the dark or in a subdued light. They will be ready for the butcher in six or eight weeks.

Bull Calves

intended to be kept as bulls also require plenty of new milk, and as they grow older nurse cows are sometimes given to them. This is, however, only done in special cases.

Ordinary Weanling Calves.

As a general principle, liberal feeding is to be preferred to hard keeping, but when calves are intended for grazing on poor land, and to be reared for cows or steers, it is not advisable to pamper them. Of late there has been a growing practice to fatten steers at a year or fifteen months old, and to produce what has been named "baby beef." When this system is carried out, they are allowed a full supply of milk from the first, and as much oil-cake and forcing food as they can eat. In more ordinary cases cattle are not put up to feed until they are about two-and-a-half years old, and run during their first, second, and third summers upon medium or poor pastures. In such cases it is not advisable to feed them highly when they are calves, but only to keep them in a healthy growing condition.

Many good farmers allow their weanling calves to suck for the first week, while others take the calf away, as already mentioned, and bring it up entirely by hand. As this system requires to be explained, we will follow the calf during its first few weeks of life, until it is old enough to be turned out to grass. We shall suppose it to be born early in February. It is first placed in a calf-pen, rubbed dry, and covered up with dry straw. About a pint of its mother's milk, called at that stage *colostrum*, is then placed in a clean basin, and the attendant proceeds to give the young animal its first lesson in the art of drinking. Two fingers are introduced into its mouth, and the calf at once begins to suck. The mouth is gently lowered into the basin, and the calf soon learns to suck up the milk. The object of the teacher is to gradually withdraw the fingers until the calf learns to drink without them. Calves of tender age are for this reason called "finger calves." For the first day or two the calf requires feeding every three or four hours, and up to the end of the first week three times a day. Afterwards twice a day will suffice.

The full allowance for a calf is eight quarts of milk a day, and this limit is reached when it is about ten days old. The following table will give a fair idea as to the times of feeding, and the quantities of milk required in order to bring up a calf :—

1st day 1 pint every three or four hours.
2nd „ 1 quart morning, 1 quart noon, 1½ quarts night.

Day	Morning		Noon		Night	
3rd „	1½	„	1½	„	2	„
4th „	2	„	1	„	2	„
5th „	2	„	1	„	2	„
6th „	2½	„	1	„	2½	„
7th „	2½	„	1	„	2½	„
8th „	3	„	0	„	3	„
9th „	3	„	0	„	3	„
10th „ to end of first month.						
	4 quarts morning	0	„	4	„	
2nd month	4 „ (old milk)	0	„	4	„ (old milk).	
3rd month	4 „ (old milk)	0	„	4	„ (old milk).	

Calves soon learn to eat a little hay, meal, and finely ground linseed-cake, and, this being the case, it is not necessary to increase the amount of milk beyond eight quarts per day, and at twelve to fifteen weeks old the calf may be weaned.

The system of weaning on milk may be considered by some persons as expensive, and other fluids are, therefore, employed. *Lactina* was a preparation invented by Mr. T. Bowick, of Bedford, consisting of finely ground meals, compounded with great care, and sold in bags. *Lactifer* is prepared by Messrs. Thorley, and is of similar character. Ayre's and Simpson's calf meals are foods of the same description, and all are well adapted for their purpose. The meal is well stirred in a little cold water, and boiling water is poured over it, the whole being well stirred. Cold water is then added in sufficient quantity, and according to printed directions sent out by the makers. Calves may be weaned very successfully upon these artificial foods.* Finely ground bean-meal may be similarly used, and with equal success.

Boiled linseed gives a pleasant-flavoured mucilage, well suited for young calves when mixed with an equal quantity of milk. Iceland moss may be boiled in water for the same purpose. All of these substitutes for milk may be used in calf-rearing with advantage, and the milk thus saved may be more profitably disposed of. Calves should be kept in roomy, well-ventilated, and well-drained houses, and supplied with plenty of bedding, so as to keep them clean and sweet. It is not advisable to tie

---

* All calf meals are rich in nitrogenous matter, obtained by the free use of beans, lentils, and lupine-meal, together with ground malt, maize-meal, locust-beans, and other ingredients. Some of them are baked, and afterwards ground up into a fine state.

them up, as they are happier free. Calves which are treated in the manner indicated are seldom troubled with illness, and at twelve or fifteen weeks old, or as soon as the weather is warm enough, may be turned out to grass.

Calves during their First Summer.

Supposing a calf to be dropped early in February, it will be old enough to turn out to grass about the middle of May. A small paddock near the homestead is the most suitable place, and it should be shaded with trees or be furnished with a shed, and there must also be a good supply of water. In practice it is found that calves intended for weaning should be born in November and December.

But little management is required further than general supervision until the end of September, when one pound of linseed-cake may be given to each calf every day. As the nights become cold they may be brought into yards.

Calves during their Second Winter.

They are now called *Stirks*, and when they are one year old are also termed yearlings. Stirks, or yearlings, are best kept in well-littered and well-sheltered yards. There they are supplied with refuse hay from the horse stables, a few sliced roots, and two pounds each per day of mixed barley-meal and cake, with straw and water. It is bad policy to starve young stock, and it is wiser to err on the side of feeding them well than to go to the opposite extreme.

Management of Yearlings and Two-year-olds.

Yearlings remain in winter quarters until about the 1st of May, when they are again turned out to grass, usually on the poorer classes of grass land, in woods, marshes, and commons, or in young plantations of trees. Here they increase in size and value until November, when they are again brought into yards, and receive similar treatment to yearlings, but with three pounds per head of meal and cake instead of two pounds. They again go out to grass as two-year-olds, and in October are either brought in for fattening or are sold to farmers who make a business of winter-feeding bullocks. The usual price of bullocks of this age is from £13 to £14 each. The management here described may be considered too expensive by some farmers. It is quite usual practice to feed entirely on the natural produce of the farm instead of giving cake. Much depends upon the quality of the pasturage, for it is evidently unadvisable to feed in winter on a scale which the summer grazing is not able to carry on or support.

Fattening of Cattle.

Well-grown steers and heifers in fairly good condition require about five months to fatten. If fairly fed, those put up about the middle of October are sold out during March and April, and practically require the whole of the winter before becoming ready for the butcher. Thus most graziers fatten one lot of bullocks, unless they are brought in in forward condition, in which case two lots may be fattened during one season.

The subject of fattening cattle is a very important one, upon which much has been written. The process is properly named "fattening," for it consists in the accumulation, or storing up, of fat. This may appear to be an unnecessary remark, but it ought to be kept well in mind, and examined closely. A lean animal, when first put up to fatten, is composed of the organs of the body, such as the stomach, intestines, lungs, heart, liver, etc.; also of the bony framework or skeleton, with muscles, tendons, a little fat, skin, blood, and a considerable percentage of water. When such an animal is put upon good keep it speedily alters. It gains weight rapidly: that is, at the rate of about two pounds every day. It becomes sleek in the coat, rounded in outline, soft to the touch, and the bony portions become thickly covered with flesh. There is at the same time a large quantity of inside fat laid up around the kidneys and intestines, and the animal is at length pronounced to be fat.

The changes which have taken place consist, first, in a portion of the water disappearing in favour of fat. Not only is fat laid up in a layer on the outside of the carcase just below the skin, but every part of the lean or muscular part of the animal becomes interlarded with fat. Unless the animal is growing, there is no great increase in the lean or muscle, and yet the weight and volume of the lean meat is increased. A well-fed piece of lean meat is found on analysis to be charged with fat, which surrounds every fibre, and causes the entire muscle to swell up and occupy more room. The meat becomes soft, juicy, and tender, owing to the large quantity of fat it now contains, instead of being hard and stringy, as would be the case in the lean meat of a lean animal.

The foods best adapted for bringing about these changes are starchy and sugary foods, or oils, such as are found in abundance in barley, maize, and rice meals, turnips, locust-beans, treacle, malt, oil-cakes, palm-nut meal, and also hay, and, to a limited extent, straw. It must, however, be remembered that in all animals the body is constantly undergoing change or waste. Every part of the body is always wearing away, and being replaced by materials which are derived from the blood. Hence, although the lean meat or muscle does not increase in quantity except in growing animals, and, in fact, may diminish through fatty degeneration of the muscular fibres, it wastes, and needs to be replaced. Hence the need of nitrogenous as well as of farinaceous and oily foods. We consequently find two principal classes of food needed :—

> **Fats, oils, sugar, starch,** and **pectin** for the formation of fat, and keeping up the heat of the body. **Albuminoids** for repairing the waste of muscle and nitrogenous tissues generally, and promoting growth in young animals.

The younger the animal the larger proportion of albuminoids are needed in the food, and the older or more mature the animal is the larger proportion of starchy and sugary foods are needed.

The proportion which these ingredients of food bear to each other is called the **albuminoid ratio.** If there is 1 part of abuminoids to 5 of carbo-hydrates, the albuminoid ratio is as 1 is to 5: if there is 1 part of albuminoids to 8 of carbo-hydrates, the albuminoid ratio is 1 to 8, and so on. Oil is the most fattening substance we know of. It passes, with little or no change, into the circulation, and is stored up as oil or fat in the body. Starch and sugar are also fattening, but not nearly so much so as fat. It takes $2\frac{1}{2}$ lbs. of starch or sugar to make as much fat as 1 lb. of oil. It is, therefore, necessary to multiply the amount of oil in a food by $2\frac{1}{2}$ before it is added to the starch as sugar, in order to find out the albuminoid ratio.

Example.—If 100 lbs. of linseed-cake contain—
   24 lbs. of albuminoids,
   29 lbs. of carbo-hydrates,
   9 lbs. of fat or oil,
the albuminoid ratio is found by multiplying the 9 lbs. fat by $2\frac{1}{2} = 22\cdot5$, and adding this to the 29 lbs. of carbo-hydrates. This equals $22\cdot5 + 29 = 51\cdot5$, and the albuminoid ratio is as $22\cdot5 : 51\cdot5$, or as $1 : 2\cdot2$.

The best albuminoid ratio in foods is as $1 : 5$ or $1 : 6$. It is therefore evident that linseed-cake is too rich in albuminoids to be used alone; but when given with turnips and straw, the albuminoid ratio is reduced to the proper level, and the feeding becomes natural and wholesome.

The albuminoid ratio in pasture grass is about $1 : 5$, and this partly accounts for the high value of grass for feeding purposes. In clover it is $1 : 4$ and $1 : 5$. In barley-meal it is $1 : 8$. In hay it is from $1 : 4$ to $1 : 10$, according to quality. In turnips it is $1 : 5$ to $1 : 12$, according to ripeness and quality. In wheat-straw it is $1 : 41$. If a mixture of turnips, straw, barley-meal, and linseed-cake is used for fattening cattle, a good ratio between albuminoids and carbo-hydrates may be readily obtained. It is not necessary to do more than to follow the practice of good farmers in order to get the proper ratio between albuminoids and carbo-hydrates; because experience has taught them the best proportion in which to mix foods together.

If, for example, we take a good mixture of foods, or diet, such as may be properly given to fattening bullocks, we shall probably find the albuminoid ratio as nearly correct as may be. Such a diet might be the following :—

>4 lbs. of linseed-cake
>4 lbs. of barley-meal,
>50 lbs. of mangel-wurzel,
>6 lbs. of hay,
>10 lbs of cut wheat-straw.

Such a mixture would be sufficient for a bullock during the earlier stages of fattening; and towards the end of the period the cake and meal might be increased to 6 lbs. each, instead of 4 lbs. We shall now calculate to the albuminoid ratio of the above mixture, and in doing so show how these calculations are made :—

Food and Weight.	Carbo-hydrates, including fat multiplied by 2·44.	Albuminoids.
Linseed-cake, 4 lbs.	29 p.c. carbo-hyd. × 4 = 116·0	
,, ,,	8·9 ,, fat × 2·44 × 4 = 86·9	
,, ,,	... ...	23·8 × 4 = 95·2
Barley-meal, 4 lbs.	57 p.c. carbo-hyd. × 4 = 228·0	
,, ,,	1·7 ,, fat × 2·44 × 4 = 16·6	
,, ,,	... ...	8·0 × 4 = 32·0
Mangel, 50 lbs.	9·1 p.c. carbo-hyd. × 50 = 455·0	
,, ,,	0·1 ,, fat × 2·44 × 50 = 12·2	
,, ,,	... ...	1·1 × 50 = 55·0
Hay (good), 6 lbs.	42·1 p.c. carbo-hyd. × 6 = 252·6	
,, ,,	1·0 ,, fat × 2·44 × 6 = 14·6	
,, ,,	... ...	7·4 × 6 = 44·4
Wheat-straw 10 lbs.	31·9 p.c. carbo-hyd. × 10 = 319·0	
,, ,,	0·4 ,, fat × 2·44 × 10 = 9·8	
,, ,,	... ...	0·8 × 10 = 8·0
	Total ... ... 1510·7	Total 234·6

The ratio of albuminoids to carbo-hydrates, with fats added in terms of carbo-hydrates, is therefore as 234·6 is to 1510·7, and by division the actual ratio is as 1 is to 6·47. Now this is just what the albuminoid ratio, suitable for fattening cattle, ought to be; and we therefore conclude that a good mixture of foods, such as is approved by practice, should be found to represent a good ratio between albuminoids and carbo-hydrates.

A good food for fattening cattle and sheep must also contain a large proportion of bulky material more or less indigestible. If this is not provided, the food is too concentrated and not suited to the nature of these animals. They are ruminants, and the "cud" could not be returned and properly masticated if it existed in too small quantities.

Again, the first stomach of cattle and sheep is of large size, and is called the rumen, or paunch. It must be properly filled with bulky food to satisfy the animal's hunger, and hence hay, straw, grass, or turnips must always form important parts of a proper dietary or mixture of foods for stock. As examples of a different class of animals we may take horses and pigs. These animals have small stomachs, and thus the feeling of hunger is much more easily satisfied. Horses and pigs therefore require their food in a much more compact or concentrated form. Pigs may be fed with barley-meal alone; but to feed an ox in this way would be contrary to nature. Horses may be fed chiefly on oats, beans, and maize, with a little hay or straw; but such a diet as would be suitable for a horse would be entirely unsuitable for a cow.

Food must also contain a small amount of mineral matter to supply the waste of bone; for bone, like the softer tissues of the body, is subject to waste and repair in common with the entire body. Mineral matter for the formation of bone is present in sufficient quantities in all ordinary stock foods.

Practice of fattening Cattle.

In order that cattle may fatten profitably certain conditions must be observed. In the first place it is important to choose well-bred animals in which the disposition to lay on fat has been increased by careful breeding. The first-prize fat cattle at our great shows are always well-bred, and it is mere waste to attempt to fatten ill-bred stock. This is a point of great importance, and should always be observed. Cattle may be fattened almost from birth; but when they are growing as well as fattening, fat is not so rapidly laid on, and the profit is derived from the general increase of the animal in size and weight, as well as from the accumulation of fat. Perhaps the best age is about three years. They must be comfortably housed, either in small yards furnished with sheds, or in covered yards or cattle-boxes containing one animal each. They are also sometimes tied up by the neck in long rows, or in stalls.

This last is a good system, provided the animals are well kept and groomed; but it is not to be recommended when the cattle are kept dirty. They cannot lick themselves or choose their lair. Their hoofs grow to a great length, and require paring, and the animals suffer from want of exercise during the months in which they are confined to one spot.

When store cattle are first brought in for fattening the change of food must be gradual. They have been

MANAGEMENT OF CATTLE.

grazing in open fields, and a change on to such feeding as was recommended a few pages back would disorder their systems. White turnips, with 2 lbs. of oil-cake and straw, are sufficient for the first week or two, and the amount of rich foods, such as oil-cake and meal, ought to be gradually increased.

Taking a medium-sized bullock as an example, we should consider the following system reasonable and according to good practice :—

First fortnight—
    56 lbs. of white turnips,
    2 lbs. of linseed-cake,
    6 lbs. of hay,
    Straw and straw-chaff to satisfy the animal's hunger.

Second fortnight—
    56 lbs. of white turnips,
    2 lbs. of linseed-cake,
    2 lbs. of barley-meal,
    6 lbs. of hay,
    Straw and straw-chaff as before.

Third fortnight—
    56 lbs. of white turnips,
    3 lbs. of linseed-cake,
    3 lbs. of barley-meal,
    6 lbs. of hay,
    Straw and straw-chaff as before.

Fourth and fifth fortnights—
    56 lbs. of Swedish turnips,
    4 lbs. of linseed-cake,
    4 lbs. of meal,
    6 lbs. of hay,
    Straw and straw-chaff as before.

Sixth fortnight—
    56 lbs. of Swedish turnips,
    5 lbs. of linseed-cake,
    5 lbs. of barley-meal,
    8 lbs. of clover hay,
    Straw and straw-chaff as before.

Seventh fortnight—
    56 lbs. of swedes or mangel-wurzel,
    6 lbs. of linseed-cake,
    6 lbs. of barley-meal,
    8 lbs. of clover hay,
    Straw and straw-chaff as before.

Towards the extreme end of the fattening period it is usual to feed still more liberally. In some cases 18 lbs. of cake and meal have been given; but 14 lbs. is a better maximum. As cattle approach the condition of prime beef they make less use of their food, and a larger proportion of it passes through the system into the manure. Thus the dung of fat animals is richer than that of lean ones, and a larger proportion of the valuable parts of the food are recovered in the form of dung. And yet it must not be thought that the food is in any way wasted during the last stages of fattening.

During the early stages the fat is mostly laid up in the inside of the animal, around the kidneys and intestines. Later, the flesh begins to thicken, and the animal to look fat and to attract the butcher's eye. Half-fattened animals are always sold at a loss, because they are not prime; and hence the last month often increases the value in the market more than any previous period.

Regular feeding and a proper arrangement as to meals is as important as is the food itself. Fattening animals should not be kept waiting for their food, but should receive it at stated times, so that they may lie down to rest and ruminate. They should be fed early in the morning and the last thing at night, as well as throughout the day. The times and methods of feeding vary a good deal, but the principle is rather that of "little and often" than thrusting large quantities of food upon animals and leaving them to breathe over it and tire of it. When cattle are being fed for show, the remnants of each meal are removed and given to younger and less valuable stock, and the mangers are thus kept clean and free from taint. The following system we know to have been practised with good results. It errs perhaps on the side of being somewhat complicated, and one or two of the meals might be omitted. Still, it is a good system, and very well shows the care with which fattening animals ought to be treated:

At 5.30 to 6 a.m., a little meal mixed with straw-chaff, and just enough pulped roots to moisten the chaff.
At 7.30 to 8 a.m., sliced roots.
At 9.30 to 10 a.m., meal and chaff as before, with pulped roots.
At 12 p.m., oil-cake, with chaff.
At 2 to 2.30 p.m., meal and chaff as before, with pulped roots.
At 4 to 4.30 p.m., do.   do.   do.
At 6 p.m., hay.

It is also a common practice to give a little hay to fattening cattle at 8 o'clock at night, to eat during the night.

The remaining points of good management consist in allowing a full supply of fresh water at all times, and in keeping the animals well littered and quiet. Noises, too much light, draughts, foul air, and everything which tends to disturb or render the animal uncomfortable, should be avoided. Restless or quarrelsome animals should be removed and placed in loose boxes, or tied up by the neck in stalls. If all the above points are attended to, we believe that the fattening of bullocks will be carried on in the best possible way.

Profits from fattening Cattle.

The profit depends principally upon the way in which

the animals are bought in and sold out. When lean stock is cheap in autumn, and beef sells at a good price in the spring, fattening may be very profitable; but when the opposite conditions occur it may be a losing business. A farmer who possesses the faculty of buying well and selling well often makes money while his neighbours are losing. The actual balance between the cost of food and attendance and the value of the animal's increase in weight is very small, and may even be on the wrong side. Hence Sir John Lawes, many years ago, gave his opinion that the increase in the case of fattening cattle is obtained at a loss; that is, when the food given and the beef sold are taken at standard prices. From what has been said, however, it will be seen that the fluctuations in the prices of feeding stuffs, of lean stock and of fat stock, give opportunities for profit which a good business man will watch. The profit of fattening cattle is not to be measured by a simple calculation as to a standard price for cake and a standard price for beef, but depends upon the prime cost of the bullock, the adaptation of the foods given to the market prices, bringing out the cattle at the proper time, and a good sale.

Another item is the value of the manure produced. The profits of bullock-feeding may be small or may be eaten up in expenses, but the manure is worth a great deal. If the business is carried on so that the cattle clear their expenses, and leave the dung for nothing, many farmers are satisfied. A fattening bullock will leave one ton of manure every month, worth about 12s. a ton, and thus during five months it leaves in manure a value of £3.

CHAPTER III.

DAIRY MANAGEMENT.

Management of Milking Cows in Winter.

We have already seen that the practice of spring calving and summer milking is general and profitable. By this system the cows are dry during most of the winter, and their food is cheap and simple. To keep up the flow of milk during winter is much less profitable than summer dairying, and the question which may occur to any one not acquainted with farming business might readily be—Why do it?

The requirements of the new milk trade render a winter supply of milk necessary; and hence, in making their contracts with farmers, milk-buyers insist upon an equal supply both in summer and winter. Gladly would the farmers escape this condition, but as business cannot be transacted without it, they make the best bargain they can, and always receive a better price per gallon for their winter's milk than for that produced in the grazing season. Hence they keep what is called a "running" dairy, or a dairy in which cows are calving at intervals throughout the year, instead of at one period, as in cheese-making dairies.

The winter management of dairy cows is not very different from that of fattening bullocks. Both are well supplied with rich foods, and the expense of keeping a cow in milk during winter is much the same as that of maintaining a fat bullock. The foods chosen are those most suited for producing a large quantity of milk, and the richness of the milk, provided it is sufficient to pass muster, is only of secondary importance to the seller.

Supposing it is desired to supply milk from October to April, the cows will gradually be put on to winter keep as the nights become colder and the grass loses its nourishing properties. The change is made slowly, and in accordance with the season. About the middle of October the cows will be housed at night, and hay will be allowed nights and mornings. Early in November about 4 lbs. per head of cotton-cake will be placed in the mangers for the animals when they come in to be milked. During November the food assumes more and more a winter character, until towards the latter part of the month the change is completed.

The best descriptions of food for cows in milk during winter are hay, silage, brewers' grains, white turnips, mangel-wurzel, cotton-cake, rice-meal, and cut straw. On many dairy farms hay is an important food, but on others only a small allowance of this material is given. For keeping up a good supply of milk we recommend:—

> 35 lbs. of white turnips or mangel-wurzel,
> 6 lbs. of cotton-cake (undecorticated),
> 40 lbs. of silage,
> ¼ part of a bushel of brewers' grains,
> 6 lbs. of hay,
> Straw-chaff,

with a good supply of clear and good water. About two bushels of a mixture of pulped roots and chaff will be found sufficient in bulk for an ordinary-sized cow, and the cake may either be mixed in with their food or given separately.

The routine of feeding consists in giving a little hay before milking, and immediately afterwards a bushel of the chaff and pulped roots, with or without the cake. The cows are then turned out for water and exercise, while the stalls are cleared of dung and wet straw. At eleven o'clock they can have their silage, and at three o'clock another allowance of chaff and pulped roots. At six o'clock they can have their hay, and this will end the day's feeding. The quantity of straw-chaff must be regulated according to the appetites of the animals, and a more liberal amount of cake may be bestowed on the animals which yield the largest quantity of milk. When grains are used, they also may be mixed with the chaff and pulped roots.

Preparation of the Food.

In large dairies a powerful chaff-cutter, driven by steam, and mills for breaking cake or grinding barley, are necessary. The straw is cut and stored in a suitable shed, and the roots are pulped daily. The food is mixed on a cemented or concrete floor, by putting down the necessary amount of straw-chaff, and scattering over it the allowance of meal and cake. The pulped roots are then thrown over the heap, and three or four buckets of cold water are added. The heap is then turned over with forks until the various parts are well mixed, and the food is given in bushel baskets to the cows in their mangers. If six hours elapse between mixing and feeding, the heap heats and has a pleasant flavour, which the cows enjoy; but it is not desirable to allow the heaps to remain too long, as it then becomes sour. The best arrangement is a long shed divided by a brick wall into engine-house and feeding-room, with a floor above for the cake-breakers and corn-mill. A shaft extends along the length of the building, bracketed to the wall, furnished with pulleys or sheaves for working the various implements, such as pulper, cake-mill, corn-mill, chaff-cutter, and pulper. The pulper may, however, with advantage, be worked with a separate horse-gearing, as it is not worth while getting up steam every day for this purpose.

Effect of Food on Milk.

The yield of milk in cows is an hereditary and personal quality. It is less affected by the food the animal eats than by the natural tendency to produce milk which she possesses. In other words, a good milker will become lean and wretched-looking, whereas a bad milker will become fat and sleek. Poor feeding will lower the yield of milk, simply because the cow must have the material for making milk, and good feeding will, on a similar principle, increase the flow up to the full bent of the cow's powers. No feeding will, however, make a good milker out of a bad one, and a good milker will go to skin and bone sooner than lower her yield. The quantity of milk is therefore in some degree dependent on liberal feeding. The quality of the milk is much less easily controlled, and it is doubtful if any special feeding will materially alter the percentage of butter fats or cream in milk. Jersey cows have been known to yield rich milk even when fed on straw;

and there is no doubt that the richness or quality of milk depends much more upon breed and individual peculiarities than upon the food given. Rich fatty foods, such as linseed-cake, do, to a certain extent, give richness to milk, but only by supplying the cow with material which she is ready to convert into cream. Cows which naturally yield poor milk will lay the fat thus given them on their backs. Let it then be understood that the best way of obtaining rich milk is to keep cows which naturally yield rich milk and feeding them well, and that it is useless to keep cows of a poor sort, and try to increase the richness of their milk by feeding them with rich food. The same is true of cows kept for cheese-making. Ayrshire cows naturally give milk rich in casein or cheesy matter, and most cows yield a fair return in cheese; but no system of feeding will greatly alter the amount. Watery foods, such as silage, grass, grains, and distillery wash, increase the quantity of milk, but lower the quality, and in town dairies, where a large amount of milk is the principal object, they are much employed.

Milk easily affected by its Surroundings.

Milk is an exceedingly delicate substance, and may be injured even before it is drawn. Bad air, bad smells, bad water, and musty or badly-flavoured food, affect milk unfavourably. Hence it is of great importance that cows should be kept in wholesome, airy, and clean houses, and be supplied with good food and pure water. Turnips and silage, if given in too large quantities, flavour the milk, and bad odours readily impart themselves to milk and butter made from it.

After milk is drawn from the cow it at once begins to change. Warm milk is, however, much less easily injured than when cold, because milk just drawn from the cow, being hot, throws off the air. The air is rendered lighter when it comes in contact with the warm surface, and flies upward, so that there is less risk of injury. In the case of cold milk the conditions are reversed. The moisture in the air becomes condensed upon its surface, and any impurities find their way into the milk and pollute it. The larger the surface exposed the greater is the risk of contamination, and hence one of the best reasons for the deep setting of milk used in the newer systems of raising cream. It will also be seen that pure air in the dairy is of greater importance than pure air in the cow-house.

Separating Cream from Milk.

This brings us to the important consideration of separating the cream from the milk.

The composition of cow milk, as ascertained by analysis, is as follows:—

Water	87	per cent.
Albuminoids (casein)	4	,,
Fat (butter)	3·7	,,
Sugar	4·6	,,
Ash	0·7	,,
	100·0	

These are the actual proportions of the various materials contained in milk, but they do not give a correct idea of the amounts of butter or cheese which milk is capable of yielding. The best butter contains a little water, and rich cheese contains nearly all the fat as well as the casein, besides water and mineral matter. One hundred parts of ordinary milk will yield 5 per cent. of butter, and if made into cheese it will yield 10 per cent. of fresh curd.

The fat of milk exists in the form of minute globules of about $\frac{1}{4440}$ to $\frac{1}{5520}$ of an inch in diameter. A single pint of milk contains about forty thousand millions of them. Their outer envelope is said to be albuminous, and the casein is dispersed throughout the fluid. The sugar of milk, or lactose, is an important element, and is highly nutritious. Milk is, in fact, a wonderfully constituted food, especially adapted for young animals. It contains fats, sugar, albuminoids, and mineral matter from which bone may be formed.

The separation of the cream was, until very lately, done by the simple principle of gravity. The watery or serous portion of milk is the heaviest, and bears downwards, whereas the more buoyant or fatty portion gradually rises to the top. The milk is spread in large flat vessels about four inches in depth, and in twenty-four hours most of the cream has risen, and may be skimmed off the surface. This system is still the most generally followed, but is open to the following objections:—

It is slow, and the milk often turns sour before all the cream has risen.

It is liable to contaminate the milk and the cream, by exposing a large surface to the action of germs which float in the air.

It is incomplete, and allows a part of the cream to remain in the milk.

In order to do away with these disadvantages, various systems have been devised. Two principles are kept in view : first, the exposing of a smaller surface to the air; second, the regulation of the temperature by means of hot and cold water or ice. It is found that cream rises most rapidly in a falling temperature. By warming the milk up to 100° Fah., and then allowing ice-cold water to flow around the vessels containing it, the milk is quickly cooled. Now, all substances and all fluids contract when cooled, but not equally. The fat globules contract much less easily than the watery portion of the milk, and hence they are rendered still more buoyant, and rise with greater speed. On this principle the Speedwell Creamer throws up the cream in three or four hours, thereby giving a fresher and

Fig. 14.—SCHWARZ DEEP-SETTING TIN.

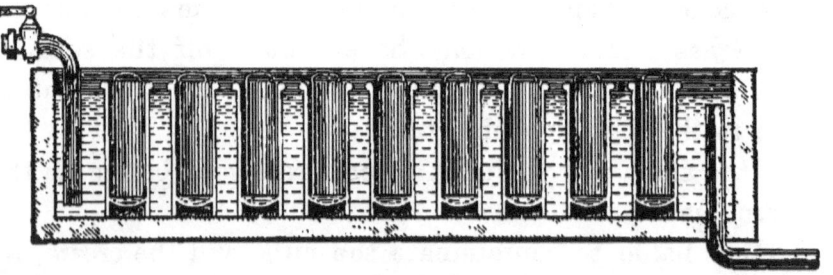

Fig. 15.—LONGITUDINAL SECTION, SHOWING SCHWARZ DEEP-SETTING TINS PLACED IN THE TANK WITH WATER FLOWING ROUND THEM.

sweeter cream, as well as saving time and (what is also a consideration) room.

The general form of the deep setting tins is oval or

circular, and they are also furnished with covers to still further protect the milk from the air. These deep tins are placed side by side in a wooden cistern lined with lead, and in this hot water is placed so as to raise the temperature of the milk. When this has been done, cold water is allowed to flow in, and the consequence is a rapid cooling of the milk and quick rising of the cream. Such is the principle

Fig. 16.—SPEEDWELL CREAMER.

of the Schwarz and Coolley methods, and in a modified form of the Dorset and Jersey Creamers. The Speedwell Creamer, which has been already mentioned, is a tin vessel in which the bottom is composed of five fangs, or finger-like tubes, which are hollow inside, and filled with milk.

(*See* Fig. 16.) By this means the hot milk is brought into close contact with cold water. A tin scoop accurately fits the upper portion of the vessel, by which the entire cream

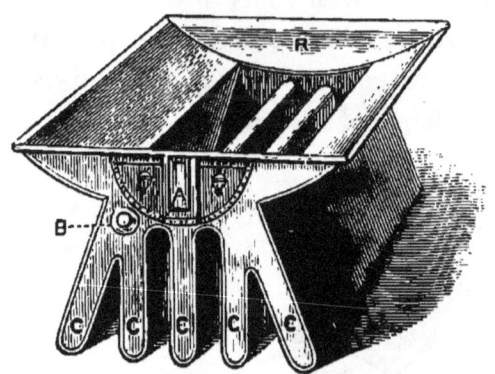

Fig. 17. - SPEEDWELL PATENT RAISER.

can be removed at once by a turn of the wrist. The Coolley and Schwarz systems are also shown in figures.

The Laval Separator

is one of the most remarkable inventions of modern times. It had long been known that centrifugal force might be employed to effect separations between substances of different specific gravities. A rapidly revolving drum, set in motion by a band driven from an engine, is the means employed. About 7,000 revolutions per minute represents the speed of the drum when in full work. The milk is allowed to run in at the centre of the drum while working at full speed. The immediate effect is that the heavier parts of the milk are thrown outwards to the sides of the vessel, and the lighter portion (the cream) remains in the middle. This is the principle of the **Laval Separator**, and the remainder of the process

DAIRY MANAGEMENT. 59

is mere detail. A slit is provided for the escape of the skim-milk, which then flows along a tube, and is delivered into a receiver. The cream escapes at an opening near the centre, and flows into a second vessel, and the separation is thus effected immediately and continuously. One hundred and fifty gallons of milk can be passed through a Laval Separator in one hour, and a larger size is made which can

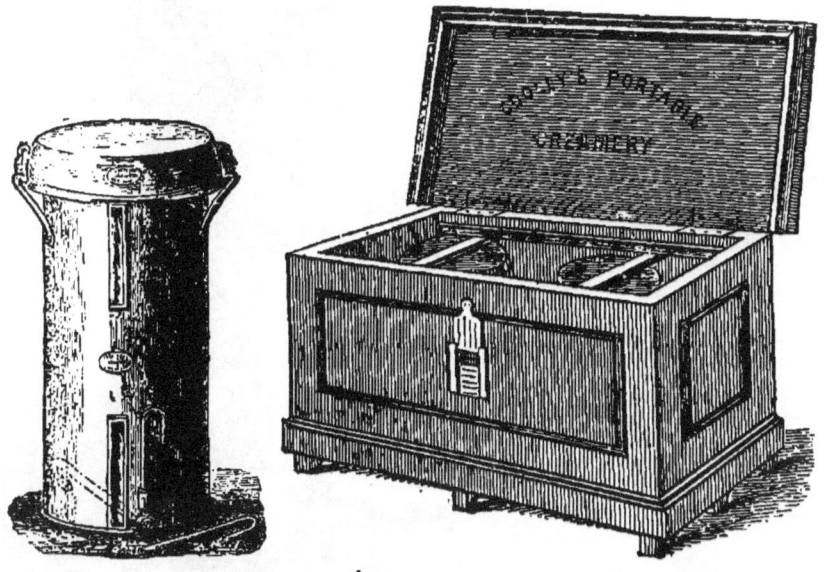

Fig. 18.—SHOWING COOLEY'S DEEP-SETTING CAN, AND TANK FOR RECEIVING IT.

separate 250 gallons in the same time. The accompanying sketch will give a very fair idea of the construction of this instrument.

The Laval Separator is more adapted for large dairies and town depôts for milk than for ordinary farm use. It requires steam power, although there is a small one now made which can be worked by hand, called the "baby separator." Where used, the separator is found to make a much more complete division of milk and cream than any other method. It ensures absolute freshness in the

Fig. 19.—LAVAL CREAM SEPARATOR.

cream, and perfect sweetness in the skim-milk. It also takes up much less room in a dairy than the large flat leads or vessels used for separating milk. These advantages, together with the rapidity of the process, render the separator a most valuable addition to the appliances of a large milk business, and it is probable that before long it will be adapted for more general use in farms.

The most recent improvement is the invention of what is called the Instantaneous Butter-maker. In this instrument a small churn is attached to the separator, and the cream passes straight into the churn, and is made at once into butter. In this case the churn consists of a small hollow cylinder, furnished with beaters, to which a rapid revolution of 3,000 per minute is communicated by means of a steam turbine. The result is an almost immediate production of butter, which keeps pace in its formation with the delivery of the cream from the separator. This wonderful invention was exhibited for the first time at the principal agricultural shows of 1890.

Butter Making.

Butter is made by agitating or shaking cream until the fatty globules break up and unite together in masses.

The art is very ancient, as may be seen by the constant references to butter in the Scriptures. It is so simple that it must have early reached perfection, and there is no reason for thinking that the butter now made is better than that which Jael set before Sisera, the captain of Jabin's host. Good butter has, however, always been rare, on account of carelessness in its manufacture. The process is simple, but success depends upon attention to details from (or even before) the time the milk is drawn from the cow to the moment when it is put on the table.

We have already seen that bad feeding, bad air, and impure water affect milk before it is taken from the cow, and that as soon as milk is cold it becomes liable to be

62 *LIVE STOCK.*

injured. The fat is the most delicate portion of the milk. Fats absorb odours very quickly. Fat will extract the smell of flowers, and is employed for this purpose in the manufacture of *attar* of roses and other scents. If, then, milk, cream, or butter is in contact with putrid smells, game, meat, paraffin, etc., it will absorb and retain their odour and flavour. This fact shows the importance of strict cleanliness and sweetness in every stage of butter-making and of milk management. A perfectly clean and sweet dairy is, therefore, a first consideration.

The Dairy

should open to the north, and ought to be protected from the sun by trees, or by a roof specially fitted or prepared to keep out the heat. It is generally a square or oblong room, with a cemented or hard-tiled floor of non-porous character. No crevices or cracks should be seen in a

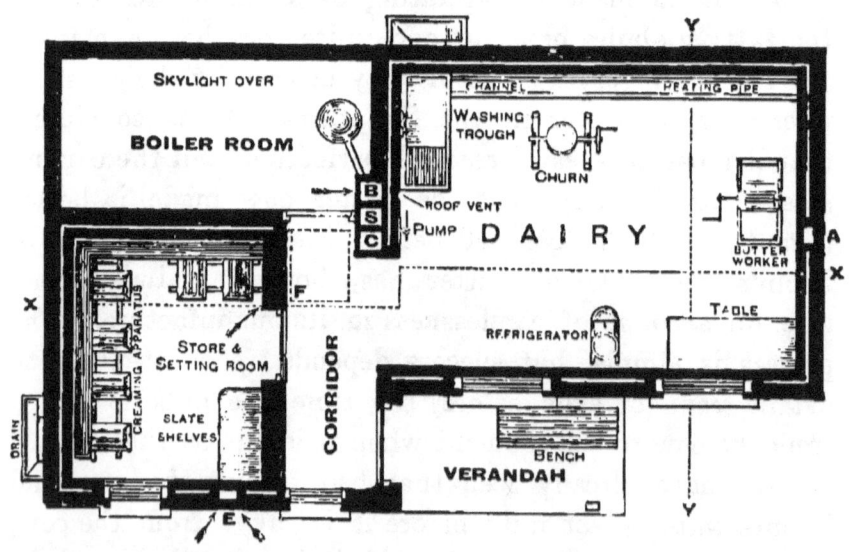

Fig. 20.—SHOWING PLAN OF A MODERN DAIRY.

dairy floor, as they only harbour sourness in some form. The walls should be whitewashed or be lined with white encaustic tiles, well fixed, and pointed with cement. The ceiling must be lime-washed and clean. The vessels for holding milk must be of porcelain, glass, lead, tin, glazed earthenware, slate, or marble: that is, of non-porous and clean character. The wooden bolls, tubs, buckets, etc., should be of oak or maple, and must be well washed in cold water, and scalded, before and after use, on all occasions. A dairy is, in a word, scrupulously clean and pure. It must be abundantly supplied with well water, and the mop or squeegee is in constant use to take up any drop of milk which may be spilt. It must also be furnished with well-trapped and well-aired drains, contrived on a simple and well-ventilated system, so as to prevent any return of impure air by this channel. Such a dairy need not be of expensive or ornamental appearance, so long as it is thoroughly clean.

The cream is raised either in shallow or deep pans, and when collected is placed in a glazed earthenware crock, in which stands a peeled willow wand, used for stirring it every now and then.

Ripening of Cream.

Butter may be made from fresh cream as it comes from a Laval Separator, and some people think that this is the best stage for churning. It is, however, a more common, and we think a better, plan to ripen cream before churning. It is a fact that sweet and good butter may be made from sour cream, and it is, therefore, very common to see cream churned once a week from slightly sour cream. By *ripe* cream we should understand cream with a slight degree of acidity, but not distinctly sour, or about three days old, and from such cream the finest quality of butter may be made. It is also considered good practice to hold back a spoonful of such sour cream, and add it to the next batch of cream to produce acidity more quickly, so that sourness in cream must not be considered a fault, provided it is not carried too far. It is of great importance that the *milk* from which cream is raised should be perfectly sweet and free from all acidity, so that sourness in cream and sourness in the milk which produces it are two very different things. Cream raised from sour milk is sure to contain cheesy matter, and this will render the butter rancid in a few days; whereas pure butter fat will keep for a long period without change.

Churning

may be done in a barrel churn or in a more modern churn, but any good churn will make good butter. The improvements in churns made during recent years are, no doubt, considerable. The old-fashioned churn (Fig. 7) consists of an oak barrel on the inner side of which two or three perforated shelves, or dashers, are fixed to agitate or break the cream. The barrel is slung upon a frame, and turned round with a winch handle. There is a large opening for removing the butter, and for pouring in the cream or water for cleansing the churn; and this is closed with a lid, and rendered tight either by a pad of cheese-cloth or by an indiarubber fitting, and kept in place by a strip of iron and a screw. There is also a ventilating peg for allowing the escape of gases, which is opened from time to time at the earlier stages of churning. Such is the old barrel churn which has long passed as a good and efficient instrument, and is to be seen very frequently even now.

Fig. 21.—HATHAWAY'S BARREL CHURN.

The faults of the old-fashioned barrel churn are as follows: First, the fixed shelves or dashers are difficult to keep perfectly clean, as they have angles in which particles of butter may cling and lodge; secondly, they are said to over-churn some of the cream and under-churn the rest. The chief action is naturally on the cream at the outside of the revolving mass, while the centre of the churn naturally moves slower; and hence it is considered that the portion of the cream nearest the centre is not sufficiently agitated.

These faults have been met by what is called the end-over-end movement (Fig. 22), in which the barrel is suspended at the bulge instead of at the ends. A diagonal

Fig. 22.—VICTORIA CHURN ENTIRELY WITHOUT DASHERS.

or swinging action has also been introduced, by which the churn revolves not only end over end, but slightly out of the centre, so that it swings to the right and left. Removable dashers fixed like a ladder between grooves within the churn are also now used, and after churning the dashers are slipped out and washed separately, while the churn is more easily washed out. Such is the Charlemont Churn (Fig. 23).

The modern system of butter-making also requires

Fig. 23.—PATENT "CHARLEMONT DIAPHRAGM" FACTORY CHURN.

glass windows at either end of the churn to admit light, and show the operator when to stop churning. Such a churn is all that can be required. There are, however, other good churns, among which may be mentioned the Plunger churn, well adapted for churning the whole milk; the Box churn, in which the outer case remains stationary while the cream is agitated with revolving beaters (Fig.

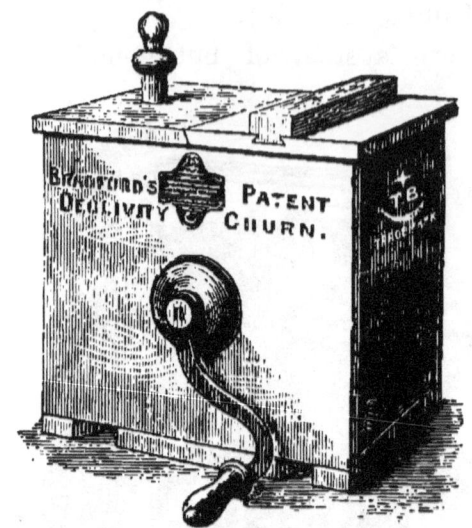

Fig. 24.—THE BOX CHURN.

24); the Cradle churn, in which the churn is made to rock

Fig. 25.—THE COTSWING CHURN ON THE CRADLE PRINCIPLE.

backwards and forwards like a cradle (Fig. 25). There are many sorts of churns, but those mentioned will give the reader a sufficient idea as to the means usually employed.

The best temperature for churning is about 60° Fahr. In winter it must be brought up to 62°, and in summer kept down to 58° by the use of warm clean water or ice, as the case may be.

When the cream is put into the churn the handle is turned slowly round about six times, and the vent-valve is then pressed down to allow the warm air and gas to escape. This is repeated until no air fizzes out, and the churning then proceeds at the rate of forty revolutions a minute. A quicker motion of about fifty revolutions may be used towards the end of the process.

Churning usually occupies from thirty to forty-five minutes, and is now stopped earlier than it used to be. The old-fashioned system was to churn until the butter

Fig. 26.—SCOTCH HANDS.

gathered into a large mass, and began to fall from side to side. It was then removed in the form of a lump, and placed in the butter tub or trendle for washing. The system now recommended is to stop churning as soon as the butter forms in small particles, variously described as about the size of pin-heads, the size of wheat-grains, or the size of vetch-seed. This is easily seen by watching the glass windows before mentioned. These are at first covered with a white sheet of cream, but when the butter is formed the particles of butter and the thinner butter-milk are to be readily seen separated against the pane.

Churning is now stopped, and the churn is turned plug downwards, and a fine hair-sieve is held under it. The plug is then removed, to allow the escape of the butter-

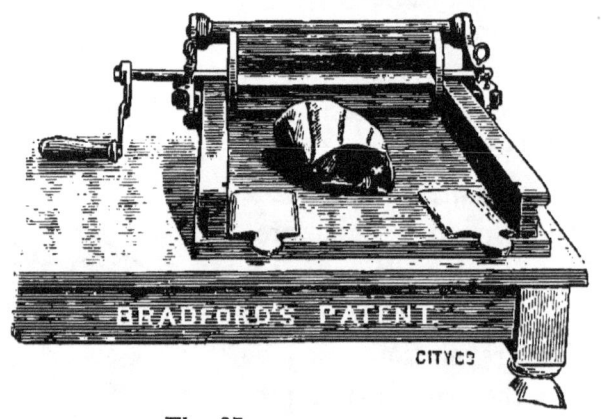

Fig. 27.—BUTTER-WORKER.

milk, and any particles of butter are caught in the sieve, and returned into the churn through the larger opening. The butter is now seen as a granular mass of rich colour lying in the churn, and on this is poured about half a bucket of pure cold spring-water. The churn is now turned round slowly about three times. The plug is again opened and the sieve again used, and the whole of the water is allowed to drain away. This operation is repeated until the water escapes almost clear, and during these washings the butter becomes a little more compact and hard. When the operator is satisfied that the butter is washed, he turns the churn slowly round in order to gather the butter into a lump, and then removes it carefully from the churn with the "Scotch hands" (Fig. 26), not allowing it to be touched by his own hands.

The butter is now placed on the butter-worker, which is shown at Fig. 27, although it may be of other forms, the

Fig. 28.—THE ALDERNEY BUTTER-WORKER.

object being to work the butter without contact with the hand at any stage. The butter-worker squeezes out all the water, and leaves the butter firm and dry. It is then worked into pats, and is ready for use.

Salting may be done either in the churn or in the butter-worker. In the former case a brine strong enough to float an egg, made by about 1 lb. of salt to 1 gallon of water, is introduced, and the butter takes up sufficient salt for flavouring. In the latter case fine dry bay-salt is sprinkled over the butter according to taste, and is worked into it uniformly.

CHEESE-MAKING

is a much more complicated process than butter-making. Anyone who follows the foregoing directions, with the assistance of an experienced dairy-maid, will soon be able to make good butter. With cheese it is far otherwise. The operations are more numerous, and are spread over a longer time. Cheese-making begins the first thing in the morning, and is not completed until evening. Great judgment is required as to the proper temperature, the peculiarities of the weather, and the time required between the various stages in the manufacture; so that good cheese-makers are rare, and uniform cheese-makers who may be relied upon to turn out a lot of cheeses of equal quality and flavour are rarer still. Cheese is made best in factories, where large quantities of milk are handled by a skilled cheese-maker, but first-rate cheese is also made in farm dairies.

To describe cheese-making is by no means easy, especially as the number of kinds of cheese is very great.

Cheese Districts.—The character of the herbage affects the quality of cheese, the best being made from land of cool and sometimes of marshy character, of medium quality, and in a natural state. Heavy manuring, draining, and other "improvements" have been known to injure the quality of the cheese produced.

Cheese is made in nearly every county, but there are districts which have become especially famous. Among them may be named the Scotch Cheddar district, in Ayrshire and contiguous counties; the Cheshire district; the West Yorkshire Dale districts; the Lancashire Dale districts; the Derbyshire Peak district; the Leicestershire and Stilton districts; the Gloucestershire Vale district; the North Wiltshire district; the Dorset district; and the Somersetshire (Cheddar) district. There are, no doubt, other localities in which good cheeses are made, but those made in the counties named have earned a particular reputation, and are in high favour.

The new milk trade has, in many localities, taken the place of cheese-making, as it is often more profitable, and always less troublesome. Of late years, however, the sale of new milk to towns has been rather over-done; and recently the price of good cheese has been high, and has caused a reaction in favour of the production of cheese. A gallon of milk may be relied upon to make 1 lb. of fresh cheese, and if 72s. a hundredweight can be obtained, this represents (allowing for shrinkage during ripening) about 7d. per pound, or 7d. per gallon of milk. Even the moderate price of 56s. is equal to 6d. per gallon on the milk, and besides, there is the whey, which is so useful for pig feeding. Now, as a great deal of milk changes hands in summer at 6d. and 7d. per gallon, it is clear that cheese-making stands at no serious disadvantage with the sale of new milk.

We can only spare space for describing one system of cheese-making, and shall select Cheddar cheese as our example, because it is widely practised, and gives a good idea as to how the process is conducted.

Cheddar Cheese-making.

The instruments required are a cheese-tub (Fig. 29), made to contain about 120 gallons of milk, a curd-knife (Fig. 30), a curd-breaker (Fig. 31), a curd-mill (Fig. 32), a cooler, or shallow wooden tray-vats (Fig. 33), and a cheese-press (Fig. 34). Besides these appliances, a thermometer, strainers, cheese-cloth, a source of pure water and of heat, and a proper shed or cheese room are required.

Fig. 29.—CHEESE-TUB AND BOILER.

Thus supplied with the necessary appliances, the cheese-maker proceeds as follows.

Cheese is made daily, and the size of the cheese varies with the amount of milk. In a dairy of 25 to 30 cows cheeses of 56 lbs. each may be made, and where 50 or 60 cows are kept cheeses are made of 112 lbs. each. The vats

DAIRY MANAGEMENT.

ought to be of sufficient size to hold two half-hundredweight cheeses, one on the top of the other.

The evening's milk is strained and put in the cheese-tub, and covered over with a canvas cloth. In the morning it is creamed, and the morning's milk added. A pailful of milk is then heated to 95° Fah., and the cream is stirred in and added to the milk in the tub.

Most cheese-tubs are jacketed, or double-cased, so that steam from a boiler can be allowed to circulate around the vessel, and the milk is raised

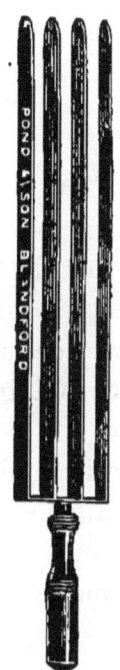

Fig. 30.—CHEDDAR CURD-KNIFE.

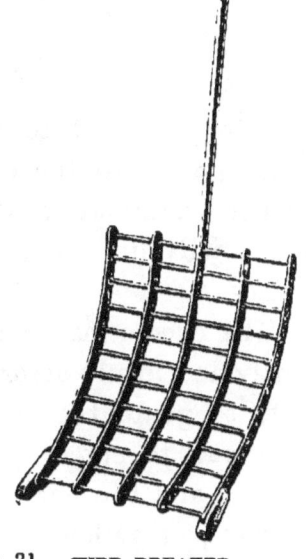

Fig. 31.—CURD-BREAKER.

to 82° Fah., more or less, according to the weather. This may be supposed to take place at 7 a.m. Patent rennet is then added at the rate of 1 oz. to 25 gallons of milk, and stirred in for five minutes. The canvas cloth is now spread over the cheese-tub and the milk is left for one

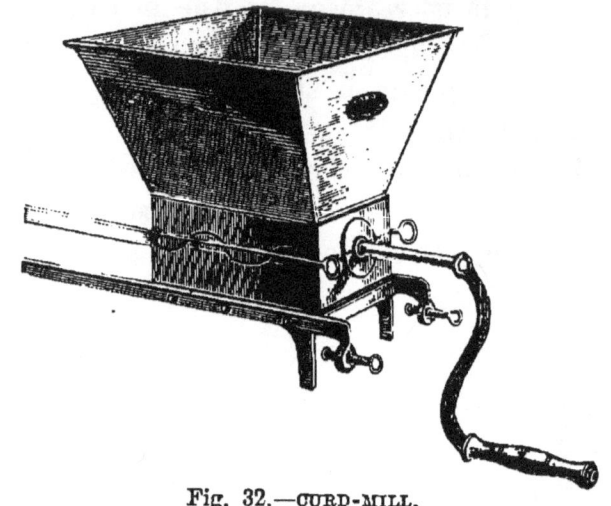

Fig. 32.—CURD-MILL.

hour for the curd to form. On removing the cloth the milk appears to the eye much as it did before; but on further examination it will be seen to have coagulated into a jelly-like mass from top to bottom, with a glazed surface.

The cheese-maker now takes the curd-knife and cuts gently and firmly across and across the curd, allowing the knife to go to the bottom at intervals of about an inch from cut to cut. He then cross-cuts it in the same manner, and the curd immediately begins to sink, and a layer of pale yellow whey appears at the top.

After an interval of twenty minutes the curd is

slowly and gently broken with the curd-breaker. The object of quick and slow breaking at this stage is to prevent the escape of the fat, for if roughly used the fat appears on the top of the whey. Steam is now again admitted and the temperature is brought up to 90° Fah., and stirring is carried on more briskly, because the curd now becomes harder and will bear rather rougher treatment. The breaking is continued for over an hour, and the temperature of the curd and whey is then raised to about 100° Fah., and the stirring is continued for a sufficient length of time to properly "cook" the curd and make it firm enough to break over the finger to the satisfaction of the maker.

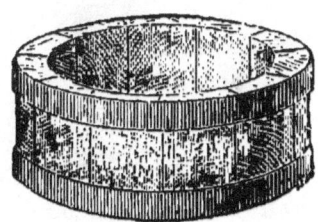

Fig. 33.—CHEESE-VATS MADE OF TIN AND OAK.

The curd is then allowed to settle or "pitch" to the bottom of the tub, and after an interval of half-an-hour the whey is drawn off.

Cheese-tubs are made with a convex bottom, and upon this the curd lies in a thick layer. When the whey is all drawn off the curd is cut in slabs of about six inches square and piled in the centre; and this cutting is repeated at short intervals to favour the escape of the whey. The curd is kept covered with cheese-cloth and a thick canvas to keep it warm between all these operations, and is now left for about half-an-hour, when it is again cut and packed close together on the cooler, being well covered up with cheese-cloth and canvas.

Cutting and turning are continued, and the curd is watched and examined, but is kept well covered to prevent it from becoming chilled. It alters to a pale drab colour and becomes sour in smell, and when it is judged to be at the proper stage of acidity and toughness it is put through the curd-mill. This may take place about five o'clock in the afternoon. Salt is then added to the crumbs of curd at the rate of $2\frac{1}{2}$ lbs. to 1 cwt., and well worked in by the hands; and the curd is then placed in the vat with a cheese-cloth nicely packed around the sides, and put under the press, and pressure is applied to squeeze out the whey. The presses are kept up to their work by occasionally turning the screws; and in the morning the cheese is turned out, a fresh cloth is put around it, and it is placed in the press again until the following morning. Thus a cheese is in the press two

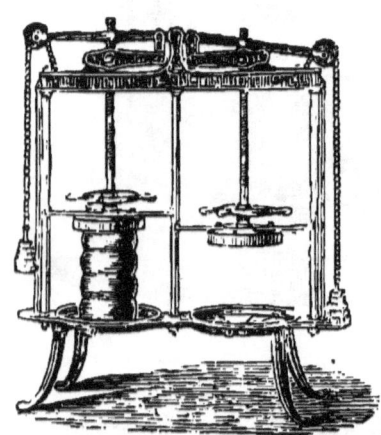

Fig. 34.—A CHEESE-PRESS.

nights and one day, and it is then removed, bound tightly in a stout canvas band made for the purpose, the ends being covered with muslin; and it is carried to the cheese-room, where it is turned daily to keep the top flat and promote equal drying and pressure throughout. Such cheeses will be ready for use in four months. The above is a short description of Cheddar cheese-making, and it will be seen that much experience and continued attention are required. The maker has to look after cheeses in all stages, and is, with his other work, kept very fully employed. When the farmer's wife and daughters make the cheese the labour imposed on the household is very arduous, as the work is repeated every day, Sundays included, from April to October.

Concluding Remarks.

We shall not attempt in this treatise to describe all the ways of making cheese. A great deal might be said upon Devonshire cream, cream cheeses, soft cheeses, Stilton cheese, Cheshire cheese, Wensleydale and Cutherstone cheeses; but this is not a treatise on dairying, but on live stock. An attempt has therefore been made to give the young reader a fair idea as to the various matters which engage the attention of pastoral farmers engaged in cattle raising.

CHAPTER IV

SHEEP.

THE sheep was the first animal ever domesticated by man. Abel was a keeper of sheep, and he brought of the firstlings of his flock to the altar as a sacrifice. There is a more or less distinct reference to the first keepers of cattle in Genesis iv. 20, where we read, that Jabal was "the father of such as dwell in tents, and of such as have cattle." Jabal was the sixth in descent in the direct line of Cain, and yet was only the "father" of such as have cattle, so that the evidence from the Old Testament favours the idea that sheep were domesticated long before cattle. The references to sheep in the Scriptures show that in the remotest times sheep were white and covered with fine wool, and the allusion to a ram caught in a thicket, as well as the use of rams' horns as musical instruments, indicate that the sheep were horned, as many of our sheep are at the present day. No one is able to say from what wild animal the domestic sheep originally came. We are naturally disposed to think that all our domesticated animals were once wild, and that they were captured and tamed by man. The horse, ass, ox, pig, dog, cat, are all believed to have originally existed as wild animals, and this being the case, it would be strange if sheep were an exception. The same appears to be true of cultivated plants. They originally grew wild, and have been chosen as useful, and cultivated until they became improved in size, appearance, flavour, and productiveness.

But the strange thing is that in several cases—of which the sheep is one—we know nothing with certainty of the wild stock from which our domestic animals and cultivated plants are descended.

Sheep bear evidence, in their wool, of very early domestication, for the wool of the sheep kept in the time of the patriarchs seems to have been fine, white, and fleecy, as it is now. Even the most accomplished naturalists are not able to throw much light upon the ancestry of sheep, and we therefore may well leave this subject to the learned, and at once proceed with the consideration of sheep as we find them.

Relation of Sheep (and Cattle) to Wild Animals

While we cannot point out any wild animal from which our sheep have been descended, we know that they, as well as cattle, are RUMINANTS, and that they therefore belong to the order RUMINANTIA, which includes all those animals which chew the cud. The whole order have many points in common. They live in flocks or herds, are timid in their nature, live on grass and green herbage, are mostly swift of foot, and are horned. The ruminants are indeed divided into families, or *genera*, by their horns.

Thus, there are hornless ruminants, of which the camel and the llama are the best examples.

The giraffe is a ruminant, peculiar for a horn covered with skin and hair, which is *persistent*: that is, never shed, and of peculiar *conical* shape.

The large tribe of deer, including fallow-deer, the roe,

red deer, etc., are peculiar for carrying spreading antlers, which are shed every year.

Antelopes have hollow horns that are never shed.

Oxen and sheep also have hollow *persistent* horns.

Oxen and sheep, indeed, are not far removed from the antelopes in their nature. Antelopes are divided as follows:—

ANTELOPIDÆ. {
True antelopes, peculiar for their lightness, agility, and beauty.
Bush antelopes, which are of clumsier form.
Ox-like antelopes, resembling oxen.
Sheep-like antelopes, resembling sheep or goats.
}

Oxen and sheep, as well as goats, appear, therefore, as genera allied to these two latter classes of the ANTELOPIDÆ.

British Sheep.

As already stated in the earlier pages of this book, Britain is rich in breeds of sheep. They are so different in appearance that they might well be considered as belonging to different species, but they are nevertheless very similar in character. The bleating of a sheep is the same, whether proceeding from a black-faced mountain sheep or a highly-bred Southdown. Their habits and nature are also the same, so that we look upon them all as *sheep*, whatever their minor differences may be.

As in the case of cattle, so with sheep: the different races may be accounted for as being caused partly by the climate under which they have been bred for long ages, as well as by the peculiarities of herbage, the fancy of breeders, and the crossing of different races. Possibly there may have been several allied races which in remote times were domesticated by man, and whose peculiarities still show themselves in their descendants. All of these causes have helped to give us many "breeds" or races of sheep.

As to horns, there is no doubt that all sheep at one time carried these appendages, but in many of our breeds the horn has disappeared, although in even the hornless kinds they occasionally appear.

The most distinctive sheep which we possess is the Scotch black-faced, or heath sheep. It has bold, compressed spiral horns, mottled black and white face, hairy wool, wild nature, and has often been remarked on as unlike any other British race. It has even been suggested that they were originally produced by a cross between sheep and goats, but there is no evidence to support this idea. They are also said to have been introduced from Spain at the time of the Armada, and it has been pointed out that they are similar to the sheep of Wallachia, in Eastern Europe. No writer can apparently do more than conjecture as to the origin of this breed, but it is probable that they were imported from abroad.

Most of the breeds of British sheep may be divided into long-woolled and short-woolled races, and mountain and forest breeds.

Long-woolled Sheep.

These carry wool of from eight to twenty inches in length, and the weight of the fleece varies from eight to twenty pounds. They are white-faced, and generally hornless: large in carcase, somewhat coarse in flesh, and are generally found on low-lying situations, although there are exceptions to this rule.

Short-woolled Sheep.

It has been said that in Great Britain we have no true short-woolled sheep. The sheep most deserving of the title of short-woolled is the Merino, which is of Spanish origin, and is found principally in France, Spain, Germany, and Austro-Hungary, from which countries it has found its way to Australia, Tasmania, and New Zealand. The wool of the Merino sheep is much finer and shorter than that of any of our races, and hence it is the true fine-woolled or short-woolled sheep. We have no wool that will compare in these respects with that of the Merino. It supplies the *clothing* wool, from which broadcloth and the finest wearing apparel are made. Our home-grown wool is known as COMBING, as distinguished from CARDING wool, and is coarse in comparison. It is employed in the manufacture of homespuns, rugs, serges, tweeds, friezes, carpets, and blankets, but cannot yield the finer fabrics.

Still, we may speak of short-woolled British sheep as distinct from the long-woolled races. Among them are included all the Down breeds, such as Sussex and Hampshire Downs. They are brown-faced, and close or short in the fleece, which is not often more than four inches in length, and weighs about four pounds. They are generally found on chalky soils, or open downs on the chalk formation in the south of England.

Forest and Mountain Breeds.

There are also several breeds of sheep of hardy and active character found on the fells and mountains of Scotland, Cumberland, Wales, and Ireland, on the moors of

Devonshire, Yorkshire, and Northumberland, all of which deserve notice.

PRINCIPAL BREEDS.

We have now made a general classification of sheep, and we must take the principal breeds in order, and give the reader a general idea as to their appearance and qualities.

1. The Leicester Breed.

We take this well-known breed first, because it was the earliest race which was definitely improved by careful breeding. Bakewell, of Dishley, has already been mentioned as a pioneer in the improvement of live stock. He took in hand the native breed of his county, and by carefully selecting the best parents for breeding, produced the Improved Leicester or Dishley sheep, which is still looked upon as one of our leading races. The work accomplished by Bakewell consisted in reducing the size, but improving the symmetry of the old Leicester. He is accused of having paid too much attention to the flesh, and of neglecting the wool; but be this as it may, he produced a sheep of wonderful merit and beautiful form, able to make the best use of its food by converting it into mutton. He also developed a very valuable quality in what is known as " earliness of maturity," or the power of producing marketable mutton several months sooner than was formerly thought possible.

The Leicester sheep is medium rather than a long-woolled, its fleece being about eight inches in length, and of fine white wool. Its face, ears, and shanks are white, and it is free from horns in either sex. Its mutton is rather coarse, and there is a disposition to lay on too much fat, which has rather prejudiced the breed of late years. The Leicester sheep has been successfully used in the improvement of all the other long-woolled races, and this has given it its greatest value in the opinion of breeders. As each breed of long-woolled sheep is mentioned, it will be seen that it owes its position in a great degree to having been crossed with Leicester sheep.

2. The Border Leicester

is a case in point. The Brothers Culley, who flourished in the latter half of the eighteenth century on the banks of the Tees, were buyers of Dishley rams, and these they crossed with the old Teeswater, long-woolled ewes. After long and careful breeding they produced an excellent flock, which they took with them down into North Northumberland, and there gave the sheep the name of Border Leicesters. In general appearance they resembled Leicesters, but being exposed to a harsher climate, and falling into the hands of a new class of breeders, they insensibly altered in character. The Teeswater blood also imparted a larger size and greater length to the carcase, and produced the difference between a Leicester and a Border Leicester which we now see. This sheep is larger and bolder in the carcase and in the features, and is highly esteemed in the Lowlands of Scotland and the border counties generally. It is largely used for crossing both with the Cheviot and the Black-faced breeds of sheep.

3. The Wensleydale Breed

must be regarded as another offshoot of the old Teeswater, and improved by the introduction of Leicester blood. It is highly esteemed in the dale districts of Yorkshire,

Lancashire, Cumberland, and Westmoreland, and may be described as essentially of Teeswater character, with a leaning towards the Border Leicester type.

4. The Lincoln Breed.

This is the largest breed of sheep in Britain, and probably the heaviest-carcased sheep in the world.

It must be allowed that at the present time the Improved Lincoln sheep is more popular than the Leicester, with which it was originally crossed.

A Lincoln tegg (yearling) will carry as much as twenty pounds of wool; and even heavier weights have often been recorded. The carcase of a Lincoln sheep has been known to scale as much as 360 pounds of mutton. It is therefore highly valuable; and it is not uncommon for a Lincoln tegg in his wool to be valued at £5. The general appearance of these sheep is white-faced and legged, and they carry a top-knot of wool on their foreheads—a peculiarity also not seldom seen in the Leicester. But the chief peculiarities of the Lincoln are its size and the mass of long wool which grows densely over the entire carcase. The wool is very dense and boldly curled. The flesh is firm and thick, and, like that of all the great long-woolled breeds, less esteemed by butchers and consumers than the mutton of the smaller breeds. The Lincoln sheep has been largely used for crossing with Merinos, to produce an animal producing a quantity of high-class wool, as well as meat.

5. Devon Long-wools.

Somerset and Devon have long been famous for their long-woolled sheep, and these have been improved by crossing, first with the Leicester, and in more recent years with the Lincoln. In general appearance and character they might almost pass for Lincoln sheep; but being separated from them by a considerable distance, they maintain their position among Devon and Somerset farmers as a distinct breed.

6. Romney Marsh Breed.

East of the river Rother, and stretching to Dungeness on the south and New Romney on the east, lies an immense tract of marsh land separated into fields by wide ditches, and supporting a singularly rich herbage. This district has long been the home of a splendid breed of white-faced, long-woolled, hornless sheep, which existed there long before the time of Bakewell.

The original Romney Marsh sheep was hardy and well calculated to resist the fogs and cold, searching winds of the English Channel. It was also adapted for grazing upon low-lying land, which, as a rule, is not suitable for sheep. The old Romney Marsh sheep was early crossed with the Leicester, with the usual effect of improving the form and shortening the time required to bring them to perfection. There seems to have been at first a disposition to uphold the old type of sheep, as hardier and better suited to the situation than the improved or crossed sheep. The Leicester was, however, successfully introduced, and the present Romney Marsh sheep is the result. The cross was effected at the close of the last century, and is now thoroughly blended and incorporated in the constitution of the breed, which has every right to be considered as a pure and distinct race. In appearance, the Romney Marsh sheep is very similar to the Lincoln.

7. The Cotswold Race.

The Cotswold Hills form an elevated table-land, extending through north and west Gloucestershire into Oxfordshire. They are highly picturesque, and in many places precipitous. The lower hills are cultivated, while the higher ranges are left in the form of open downs, or wolds. The soil is of limestone character, traversed by thick bands of clay, which give a very varied character to the land. The climate is severe and the altitude considerable, so that a hardy breed of sheep is essential to successful sheep farming. This quality is possessed in an eminent degree by the Cotswold sheep, which are considered to be more suitable to the locality than any other race. They are high standing, or a little long in the leg and neck, and carry their heads more erect than Leicesters or Lincolns, are white-faced, although a few spots of grey are not objected to. The forehead is decorated with a long and flowing lock of wool, and the ears are long and flexible. The wool is long and composed into a bold curl, and is thickly set upon the skin. The breed was improved early in the present century by crossing with the Improved Leicester, but for many years has been bred pure. It is a little lighter than the Lincoln or the Romney Marsh sheep, and fattens at ten to twelve months old to a weight of twenty-two to twenty-five pounds per quarter when fairly treated. None of the foregoing races are horned.

SHORT-WOOLLED SHEEP.

8. Southdown.

The Southdown deserves to be mentioned first among the shorter-woolled races, because it was the earliest upon which the breeder's art was exerted in the way of improvement. The unimproved races which were general one hundred years ago appear to have been very inferior animals. They were in many cases larger in frame than the improved races of to-day, but are described as long-legged, flat-ribbed, razor-backed, narrow-chested, slow-feeding, and light-fleshed. In this all writers agree.

Fig. 35.—SOUTHDOWNS (from the flock of Mr. Jonas Webb).

The Messrs. Ellman, of Glynde, near Brighton, were the improvers of the Southdown, and they appear to have left them in a wonderfully perfect form. The elder Ellman lived in the long reign of George III., and this monarch greatly admired the improvement which Mr. Ellman effected. The younger Ellman was an old gentleman when the writer met him in 1864, and he died shortly after that date. The Southdown holds a similar position with regard to the shorter-woolled or Down breeds of sheep that the Leicester holds with reference to the long-woolled races, for there is not a race of Down sheep which has not been crossed and improved by means of the Southdown. This is the most perfectly formed of all our sheep. The face is like that of a fallow-deer, and is of light brown colour, and the head is free from horns. The width between the eyes, the beauty and prominence of the eye, and the perfect symmetry of the carcase, all help to make up a beautiful little animal, which has always been a favourite, especially among land owners.

The quality of the mutton is very high, as the flesh is tender, of excellent flavour, short-grained, and dark in colour. The joints are not too large, and look well on the table.

The flesh is at perfection at four years old, but most of these sheep find their way to the butcher at from ten to fourteen months old. When grazed in parks, it is not unusual to allow them to run until they are of maturer age, and thus the table of the mansion may be supplied with four-year-old mutton rivalling the purest venison in quality. The plumpness of form and perfect symmetry of the Southdown, its short and well-trimmed fleece, its lovely head and limbs, place it in a peculiar position with respect to other breeds, and it is scarcely to be wondered at that this sheep should have enlisted the interest of the highest personages of the land, among whom may be mentioned especially the Prince of Wales, the Duke of Richmond, and Lord Walsingham, all of whom have long been associated with Southdown breeding.

9. The Hampshire Down Breed.

The Southdown Hills find their eastern limit at Beachy Head, near Eastbourne, and extend through Sussex, crossing near Arundel into Hampshire. They pass Winchester and Salisbury, when they expand into the vast plateau known as Salisbury Plain. These are the West Country Downs, which have been the home of the Hampshire Down sheep. This admirable breed is inferior to none as a profitable animal. It is larger than the Southdown, and must take, in consequence, a second position with reference to quality of mutton. What is lost in quality is, however, fully made up in quantity and earliness of maturity, for which this race is peculiarly famous. Hampshire Down lambs bear the palm for this important quality, as they can be made ready for the butcher at seven months old. In this point the Hampshire Down eclipses every other race of sheep. When well treated, a Hampshire Down lamb will increase in weight from the day of its birth until it is sold to the butcher at the astounding rate of three-quarters of a pound per day!

The Hampshire Down sheep is the result of careful breeding, and the judicious introduction of Southdown blood, over a long period. The foundation was the old Wiltshire Horned sheep, which appears to have been in some respects similar to the Dorset Horned sheep of the present day: that is, white-faced and horned. These and the old Berkshire breed, which was black or mottled-faced, Roman-nosed, and of large size, were crossed, and subsequently Southdown sheep were introduced, and gradually altered the sheep of both Wilts and Hants. About 1860 Mr.

Humphrey, of Oak Ash, was a great breeder of West-Country Downs, as they were then called, and had recourse to the best Southdowns of Mr. Jonas Webb, of Babraham, Cambridgeshire, and by judicious breeding gave a new start to the breed, which then became known as Improved Hampshire Downs.

The Hampshire Down sheep is of large size and beautiful symmetry, although somewhat coarser than the

Fig. 36.—PRIZE PEN OF HAMPSHIRE DOWN.

Southdown. Its larger, bolder, and blacker head, long and spreading ears, and ampler form, easily distinguish it from the Southdown breed. It is found in the greatest perfection within a radius of about twelve or fifteen miles of Salisbury, in the counties of Wilts and Hants, and many of the most celebrated flocks are to be found within this area. It is the custom to breed from ram-lambs, and at the annual sales as much as one hundred guineas have been often given for lambs not more than seven months old. Sixty and seventy guineas are often realised. The early maturity and quick growth of these sheep is truly marvellous. Let anyone who doubts it visit Salisbury Fair on July 15th, and inspect the pens of wether and ram lambs there exhibited.

10. The Suffolk Down.

Of late years the Suffolk breeders have taken vast pains with their native breed. This is also a large black-faced sheep, having some points in common with the Improved Hampshire Down. It is at once distinguished from this last breed by its bare head, which is covered with black short hairs, not only on the face, but forehead and poll, whereas the Hampshire breed is well covered between the ears with wool.

The Suffolk sheep-breeders were among the first to start a flock-book for the purpose of recording the pedigrees of their sheep.

11. The Shropshire Sheep.

Of late years—since about 1851—there has been a wonderful increase in the number of good breeds of sheep. Previous to that time the Royal Agricultural Society only recognised four great classes of sheep on their prize list:—

1. Leicesters.
2. Other long-woolled sheep, not Leicesters.
3. South Downs.
4. Other short-woolled sheep, not South Downs.

About the year 1851 Shropshire sheep were allowed a

separate class, and since that time a large number of other breeds have secured an independent position as separate and recognised breeds.

The Shropshire sheep is a good example of successful crossing. It appears to have sprung originally from a small speckle-faced ewe, known as the Morfe-Common sheep, and upon this foundation Leicester, Cotswold, and Southdown crosses were superadded, until a sheep was gradually formed possessing the good properties of all these breeds. During the last forty years the Shropshire sheep has been purely bred, and is now fixed in its type or character. At first sight it might be mistaken, by a novice, for a Hampshire Down, but closer inspection will show several points of difference. The ear is shorter, and more hidden in wool. The face is woolled nearer the nose and further across the cheeks, the throat is fuller, and often shows folds of loose skin. The shanks are covered with wool down to the hoofs, and the carcase is peculiarly thick. In other respects there is a great similarity to the Hampshire breed. These sheep are found in perfection around Shrewsbury, Worcester, Birmingham, Wolverhampton, Wellington, and other midland towns, and are the principal stock of Shropshire, Staffordshire, Worcester, and adjoining counties. They are frugal in their habits, and will bear hardship well. They have been imported into many countries, and even into Scotland, where they do well, and there is also a large export trade of them to various British colonies. The Shropshire breed of sheep must be considered as one of the most important, as it is widely distributed and greatly esteemed, both on account of its wool and mutton.

12. The Oxford Down.

In the period from 1850-1860 this breed was known as "Crossbreds." They originated in the union of Hampshire and Cotswold sheep, which was always a popular cross, as it combined the high quality of mutton which is peculiar to all the Down races with the weight of flesh of the Cotswold. Mr. Druce, of Eynsham, near Oxford, first attempted to fix the breed, and to make a new race, and this he did with complete success. The name of Crossbred was dropped in favour of that of the Oxford Down, by which it is now recognised. These sheep are of very excellent character, and have many admirers. They are uniformly brown in the face and legs, and carry a heavy fleece of medium length. The Oxford Down is at once recognised by its long and well-formed ear and bold head. It reminds the observer of both the original stocks from which it was derived, having the fine feature and bold nose of the Cotswold, and the dark-coloured head and fine wool of the Hampshire side. The Hampshire, Shropshire, and Oxford races are, in some respects, rivals, as all have sprung into existence during the last generation, and all are at the present time progressing in public estimation. They have, however, become still more serious rivals of the two famous breeds which at one time, and within the memory of many of us, divided the field between them: namely, the Leicester and the Southdown. If any test of agricultural progress during the last fifty years were required, no better one could be applied than the rising of these excellent breeds of sheep, and their general adoption throughout the country.

13. The Dorset Horn Sheep.

This is one of the few horned breeds. When the old Wiltshire Crock, or Crook, wandered over the Downs around Salisbury in place of the present Hampshire Down, white-faced, fine-woolled, and horned sheep must have extended from Salisbury Plain to the south coast. The old Wiltshire Crook has, however, ceased to exist, the last flock having been dispersed about 1829. The Dorset breed has met with improvers and admirers, and is now found in large numbers around Dorchester and on the Hampshire south coast, as well as in the Isle of Wight. It is a white-faced, short-woolled breed, both sexes carrying horns, although those of the females are much less than those of the rams. A Dorset ram is a fine object, with his bold horns sweeping in circles around his eyes and ears. The Dorset breed has long been used for producing early lamb for the London market. The ewes produce in October, or even earlier, and their lambs are sold fat at Christmas. The appearance of these sheep is very characteristic, and there is no other breed which could possibly be mistaken for them. They are not widely distributed, and are chiefly to be found where the mildness of the climate suits the breeding of early lambs for the table.

MOUNTAIN AND FOREST BREEDS.

14. The Heath or Black-faced Breed.

This breed has already been mentioned (page 83) as a very distinct one. It inhabits the Highlands of Scotland, and has been introduced into the mountainous tracts of

North Wales. It is the principal sheep upon the heathy lands of North Northumberland, and is found upon the moors of Yorkshire and in the Peak district of Derbyshire. Wherever grass gives way to heather, the Black-faced sheep is found to suit. In common with every other breed, the Black-faces have met with improvers, and the sheep of to-day are very superior to those of a generation since. The face is mottled black and white, and short hairs extend backwards to the poll. The horns are flat, transversely barred, and boldly turned in the males, but simply crooked in the females. The wool is long, lashy, and straight, approaching to a hairy quality, and in the less improved stocks there is a line of hair following the spine. The carcase is short and square, and the sheep are very active and hardy. They are fit denizens of the mountain and the moor, children of mist and snow, and their appearance is equally interesting whether grazing among the flowery heather or battling with the snow-storms of winter. The flesh of these sheep is of the highest quality, and often carries with it the flavour of the heather on which the animals graze. It is a good example of the fitness of our different breeds of sheep for all circumstances of soil and climate, for here we have an animal which can live where any other race of sheep would starve. The life of a shepherd upon the mountains of Argyleshire, as of Sutherlandshire, is an anxious one, and the sufferings of even the hardy Black-faced sheep during winter are severe, and accompanied with heavy mortality. The stock farms are of immense size, many of them being 35,000 acres in extent, while in some cases they reach the gigantic area of 70,000 acres. These barren tracts are mostly of black mountain ground, interspersed with a smaller proportion of green ground, and the rent is about 5d. to 7d. per acre. Two thousand breeding ewes will be maintained on 35,000 acres, and the produce is kept for three years before they are sold.

15. The Cheviot Breed.

This is a white-faced, hornless, medium-woolled race, which has for long occupied the Great Cheviot, separating England from Scotland. The sheep is well adapted for the rugged and inhospitable region it inhabits. It is slow in fatting, and requires at least twenty months to mature. The care of Cheviot flocks upon the Cheviot Hills is as full of event, and even of romance, as is the tending of Black-faced sheep on the Scottish mountains. The Cheviot shepherds are a fine race of men, who look well after the interests of their employers, with very little supervision. Cheviot ewes are often crossed with Border Leicester rams, and the produce fattens more kindly and in less time than the pure Cheviot. A large area of the border counties is stocked with first or second crosses of Cheviot and Leicester sheep. Many Lowland farmers hold a hill farm on Cheviot or Lammermuir, and keep a Border Leicester flock at home and a Cheviot flock on the hills. The half-bred "hoggs" are brought off the grazings in autumn, and fattened upon turnips.

16. The Herdwick Race.

This interesting race of sheep is found in greatest perfection in the lake district of Cumberland, Westmoreland, and North Lancashire. The rams often, but not always, carry horns. When the lambs are born their legs and heads are black, but as they grow older the dark colouring disappears, and at three years old they are perfectly white. The wool is heavy and strong, and disposed to be hairy on the top of the shoulder. The head carries a "toppin" of wool, and is broad, with a bold Roman profile. The ears are white, fine, and erect, and always moving. The Herdwick is remarkable for its hardihood, and is much valued. It has been maintained pure for many generations, and it is asserted that no cross can improve them. The chief markets for Herdwick sheep are those of Cockermouth, Penrith, and Kendal.

17. The Lonk Breed.

This is a Lancashire breed. It closely resembles the Scottish Black-faced, but the wool is distinctly finer and softer. The horns and face are similar to the Scotch Black-faced sheep. The peculiarity of the Lonk is its suitability for mossy, low-lying ground—a situation which is not fitted for sheep in general, but on which the Lonk thrives well.

18. The Crag Sheep.

This hardy breed is found on the higher moors of West Yorkshire and East Lancashire. It is a white-faced, fine-woolled race, the rams often being horned. These sheep will thrive upon the dry mountain limestone soils of the West Riding, and require no water. They are, therefore, suited for a different class of circumstances to that in which the Lonk breed thrives, thus again showing the fitness of various breeds of sheep for different situations.

19. The Exmoor Breed.

This breed is horned in both sexes, and white-faced. It is well covered with dense wool, of rather long staple, massed together after the style of Leicester wool. The close affinity with the Dorset mentioned by Youatt is not apparent now, whatever it was at the time when this excellent writer penned his comprehensive work on sheep. The Exmoor sheep is active and hardy, and yields mutton of great excellence.

20. The Dartmoor Breed.

Exmoors and Dartmoors are classed together by Youatt as scarcely distinguishable. The Dartmoor breed is, however, much larger than that of Exmoor. There is no doubt that they were crossed with the Leicester, for Youatt says: "An improved system has, however, lately (1851) been introduced with regard to the lambs: the horned ewe is crossed with the Leicester ram, and from this cross the lambs often become as large in July as the native stock used to be when they arrived at maturity."

The Dartmoor sheep exhibited at Plymouth, 1890, appeared as a large long-woolled—or at least heavy-fleeced—sheep, rivalling in size the Cotswold, Lincoln, or Romney Marsh. They were hornless and white-faced, and did not give the idea of a particularly active and forest-like breed.

21. The Roscommon Breed.

This is the most useful and popular of the Irish races. It is seen grazing on the rich limestone pastures of the sister island, and bears a striking resemblance to the English Leicester, with which it has been frequently crossed. The history of the importation of the Leicester sheep into Ireland is well given by Youatt. He says: "The new breed struggled for a while against prejudices and difficulties of every description, and at length completely triumphed." In the Roscommon sheep of to-day we have the result of this successful introduction of Leicester blood.

22. The Ryeland Breed.

The old Ryeland was said to be the only truly fine-woolled sheep of Britain, and appears to have possessed many of the features of the Merino. Until recently it was considered to be extinct as a breed, but it appears to have been kept by certain breeders through a long period, in which it was little thought of by the general farming public. When the revival of interest in all breeds set in, the breeders of Ryeland sheep bestirred themselves, and made an effort to again establish the Ryeland sheep.

The Ryelands include a tract of sandy soils, in which Ross, in Herefordshire, and the beautiful river Wye at and about Ross, occupy a central position. "The Man of Ross," whose virtuous career has been for long known and appreciated, may serve to remind of this locality, which is also well known to tourists as the site of Tintern Abbey and some lovely scenery. It is here that the Ryeland sheep found its home.

The modern Ryeland sheep is not so fine in the wool as the older type, which as a fine-woolled sheep has ceased to exist. The sheep has, however, still its admirers, and possesses many excellent qualities worthy of notice. It is early in maturing and fattens readily, and is worthy to take its place in a list of the British breeds.

CHAPTER V.
MANAGEMENT OF SHEEP.

THE management of sheep, like that of cattle, includes three principal branches—breeding, rearing, and fattening, besides treatment in disease as well as in health. We will endeavour to give in few words a general idea of all these branches. It is true that different breeds require rather different treatment, and still more do the several localities where sheep are found. Thus the treatment of a flock of Scotch Black-faces differs very much from that of Hampshire Downs in Wilts and Hants. Still, as said in introducing the different breeds, a sheep is a sheep, wherever he is found, possessing the same habits and wants, so that, after all, there is a great similarity, as well as difference, in the management of flocks.

Sheep are known by different names, according to their age and sex. When first born they are spoken of as *ram* or *tup* lambs, and *ewe* or *gimmer* lambs, and after *castration* the ram lambs are called *wether* lambs.

A *dinmont* is another name for a wether, and a *chilver* is another name for a gimmer lamb. A *hogg* or *tegg* is a year-old sheep, and the name is generally used when lambs are about ten months old. We may speak of ewe hoggs and wether hoggs, of ewe teggs and wether teggs, and also of chilver and dinmont teggs. When teggs have been shorn they are called *shearlings*, and the sexes are spoken of as shearling rams or shearling ewes. A shearling ewe is also called a *gimmer* or *theave*. Sheep are described, according to age, as shearlings, two-shear, three-shear, or four-shear, but are also commonly described as *two-tooth, four-tooth, six-tooth,* and *full-mouthed* (eight-tooth). A shearling is also a two-tooth, a two-shear is a four-tooth, a three-shear is a six-tooth, and a four-shear is a full-mouthed sheep. When sheep (ewes) pass beyond the stage of full-mouthed, the teeth often become imperfect, and they are then called *broken-mouthed*. Ewes which are drafted from the flock on account of age, or for any other reason, are called *draft ewes, cull ewes,* and *crones.*

Sheep Breeding.

When the soil and situation are favourable, sheep breeding is found to be a profitable pursuit. It is mostly carried on upon medium or poor soils, because it is not desirable that ewes should be fat, or in too high condition. The lambs may be, and generally are, sold towards the end of summer at the early autumn fairs, and find their way on to a better class of soils where they are fattened. It is also very common to breed lambs and fatten them upon the same farm. The system of breeding stock and fattening them at home is a very good one, because store or lean sheep are often so dear that the buyer finds fattening to be unprofitable, and when he rears his own lambs he is more independent of the markets. He is also less likely to be troubled with unhealthy or unsound sheep, and the profits are more certain.

Different Systems of Breeding Sheep.
Ram Breeding.

Some farmers keep high or pure-bred flocks far too valuable for killing. Their object is not to sell to the butcher, but to breeders of sheep, who buy their produce to improve their own flocks. Such sheep bring very high prices, and sometimes above £100 are given for a single sheep. Such farmers are called ram-breeders, because their principal object is the breeding of ram lambs or shearling rams, which are sold every year at an auction, and put up separately to the highest bidder.

Breeding fat Lambs.

Another class of breeders find their profit in breeding early lambs to supply the fat market. This also is a profitable industry, and a great deal of its success depends upon bringing out good lambs early in the season, when lamb is sold by the butcher at a high price per quarter. It is conducted upon good land and in favoured situations as to climate, and certain breeds—and especially the Dorset horned ewes—are kept for the purpose. Many other breeds are, however, well suited for producing fat lambs, and a cross between a down and a long-woolled sheep is good for this purpose.

Breeding Store Lambs.

But by far the largest number of flocks are kept for producing lambs, which, after running on the hill pastures during their first summer, are sold in August and September into the hands of graziers who make it their business to fatten them during the winter, and to sell them as mutton at from twelve to sixteen months old. A great deal of poor land in England, Scotland, Wales, and Ireland, which could not be profitably employed in any other way, is kept under ewes of different races, according to the climate and the character of the herbage, and such farming is also often very profitable.

Management of Ewes.

The management of a high-class ram-breeding flock is a very difficult and expensive task. It is the object of the breeder to excel, and his rivals in the business are equally determined not to be beaten. To keep up and improve such a flock, and to bring out the sale rams in tip-top condition, are objects by no means easy to achieve, requiring constant attention and a large expenditure of money, as well as the exercise of great skill. It is not probable that any short treatise on sheep could give the information needed for carrying on such a complicated and skilful business.

We shall therefore devote ourselves to the general management of an ordinary flock, but may observe that there are many points in such management which apply equally to the most valuable flocks. In fact, however good a flock may be, it is managed—so far as feeding and daily treatment are concerned—much in the same way as ordinary sheep stock. Pedigree sheep should not need to be pampered, but, on the contrary, ought to be as hardy as other sheep. The skill of the breeder is shown in selecting parents, and turning out his sheep in a perfect form before customers; but the ordinary routine management of the ewe flock does not differ in any special degree from that of other sheep.

The management of a ewe flock resolves itself into feeding and general treatment at each season of the year. The best period of the year to commence its study is just after the lambs have been weaned, as this leaves the ewes free for the next " crop " of lambs; and by following the history of a flock from weaning one year to weaning in the following year, a tolerably correct idea may be obtained of the treatment throughout the year.

When lambs are taken from the ewes, their mothers should be placed upon poor keep, partly to dry up their milk, but also because rich food is not any longer necessary. On most farms poor pasturage can be found, and the flock is also used to clean or eat up the leavings of those sheep which are being got ready for sale. Weaning takes place in May and June, or in late districts in July. As an example of how ewes are now fed, we may imagine the case of a large sheep stock, consisting of ewes and various sections of lambs. If the most forward lambs are allowed a certain area of vetches, of clover, of cabbage, or of rape, they are not made to eat their food up clean, but after they have been over it the ewes are allowed to eat up the scraps and leavings.

Thus the ewe flock is economically employed, and all waste is avoided. Running the ewes on bare pastures, and employing them as scavengers after the more pampered sheep which are preparing for market, they are carried on at little cost to harvest. After harvest they can earn a living on the stubbles, and in the grass lands about to be broken up for wheat, and thus they are carried on to the time when the rams are turned out. At this season the ewes ought to be placed on good food, so as to ensure a good fall of lambs, and for this purpose they receive a certain quantity of white turnips, rape, mustard, good grazing, and sometimes about a quarter of a pound of oil-cake. After they are seasoned they are again put on to poor keep, without any extra or bought food, such as cake and corn, until they lamb. After ewes have lambed they are gradually given an allowance of linseed cake, oats, maize, or other foods, together with hay and turnips, so as to encourage the flow of milk and nourish their lambs well. The amount of artificial food allowed depends upon the purpose for which the lambs are bred. Ewes intended to bring up ram lambs or fat lambs cannot well be over-fed, but when ordinary store lambs are required a much less quantity of corn or cake will suffice. An ordinary *maximum* quantity of cake for ewes will be 1 lb. per day each, but $\frac{1}{4}$, $\frac{1}{2}$, and $\frac{3}{4}$ lb. per head are all ordinary quantities. As a general principle, the better the ewes are fed the stronger and bigger will the lambs be, but all must depend upon circumstances. In some cases the ewes never touch corn or cake from one year's end to another.

General Treatment.

We strongly advise that ewes should be provided with plenty of dry food during winter, and especially when they are heavy in lamb. Hay and cut straw are not expensive articles of food on a farm, and these should not be spared in November, December, and January, or up to lambing time. Ewes fed with plenty of dry food are not greedy of turnips, and thus too large an allowance of turnips is prevented without in the least pinching or starving the ewes.

Another point of importance is to give them a dry lair on stubble, grass land, or down; as a wet, slippery, or sodden lair is very bad for ewes in lamb. They must not be quickly driven, or made to pass rapidly through gateways, or teased with dogs, as sometimes happens. If these rules are observed and the feeding is judicious, the flock will be brought safely through the critical time up to lambing. Much harm is often done by being too sparing in the use of hay; and especially in November, when the autumn rainfall is often severe, ewes should have one pound per day of hay, or of a mixture of hay and straw. Those who are fortunate in possessing an area of unbroken up down or of park find it exceedingly useful at this time, as it affords grazing and a dry lair for the flock.

A young Ewe Flock.

Ewes will continue to produce lambs for several years, and one instance was related to the author of a ewe breeding until she was fourteen years old. It is, however, good policy to keep the flock young. As a general rule, ewes bring their first lamb at two years old, and continue in the flock for three seasons, bringing three " crops " of lambs. They are drafted at four and a half years old, when still in full vigour, and are then at an age in which they may be bought either for fattening or for breeding. Any particularly good ewe may be kept in the flock a few years longer, and ewes which have not been satisfactory may be drafted a year sooner, so that the general average will be found to be as just stated. In a good flock it should always be the object of the master to improve it year by year; drafting should therefore be used as an opportunity for getting rid of all faulty ewes, as well as old ones. A more than sufficient number of ewe lambs should be kept to fill up the gap left in the flock after drafting, and the new comers should be a shade better than those which are going out.

The Lambing Season.

A ewe goes twenty-one weeks in lamb, and this is called the period of *gestation*. As lambing time approaches increased attention should be given to the comfort of the ewes, and a suitable lambing pen should be constructed. In some places the ewes are brought into the rick-yard every night, which is kept well littered with straw. In others a fixed and permanent lambing pen is erected, with a sleeping-room for the attendant, and a stove and boiler for the comfort of weakly lambs and for heating milk. A shed runs around the outer wall, and is divided by cross partitions into little cells, or coops, for each couple.

When lambing time falls late—that is, in April—ewes are often not brought in at all, and no provision is made in the form of a pen. Here ewes and lambs are allowed to take their chance, favoured by mild spring weather. It is, however, wiser under all circumstances to provide some shelter for young lambs and their mothers. On large sheep farms, where flocks of 500 to 1,000 ewes are common, the lambing pen is erected wherever there is the largest amount of food. It is, therefore, a temporary construction, formed of posts and rails, with straw stuffed between double rows of hurdles, and a narrow line of thatched shedding for dividing off into coops. Such a pen will occupy about a quarter of an acre of ground, and is divided by cross-lines of hurdles into several large yards, all of which are well littered with straw. A large straw stack often occupies the middle, and affords a source of food and litter, and of shelter from the wintry blast. The pen should be made upon sloping ground, with an inclination towards the south, and ought to be close to a turnip field, upon which it opens. There should also be a hay-rick at hand, and a pond.

As some of our readers will probably some day have to help in erecting such a pen, we will show them how it is done. The farmer has had this matter in his mind for several months before, and has arranged to build one or

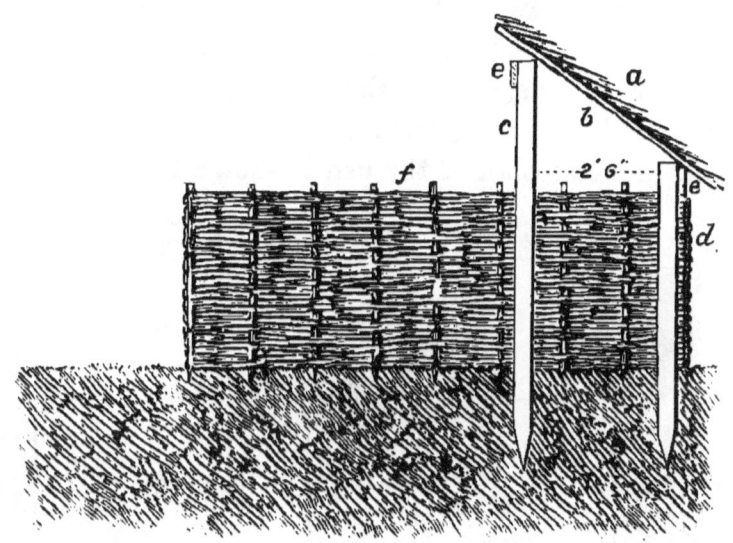

Fig. 37.—SHOWING A SECTION OF THE OUTER FENCE OF A LAMBING PEN.

a, Thatch covering; *b*, Hurdles on which the thatch is laid; *c*, Inner 8 ft. stake; *d*, Outer 6 ft. stake; *e, e*, Section of rails supporting thatched hurdles; *f*, Hurdle for dividing the shed into cells or coops.

two hay and corn stacks near at hand. The first thing to be done is to thrash the corn with a portable machine, and build a long straw rick neatly thatched down, extending from east to west, or, at all events, with a view to shelter.

The lambing pen is marked off around this rick, and eight feet and six feet posts, with rails as well as hurdles, are carted up to the site. The labour begins by driving a double row of posts about ten feet apart around the area. The six feet posts form the outside row, and the eight feet posts are driven in opposite to them on the inner side, and both rows of posts are joined along the top by a rail. The space between the six feet posts is then filled by a double row of hurdles fixed in the ground, and bound firmly to the posts. The hurdles are stuffed between with straw. A number of thatched hurdles are then placed in a sloping direction from the inner rail to the outer boundary, and thus a long shed is made. A section of the shed is shown at Fig. 37.

The general plan of the pen is shown by Fig. 38.

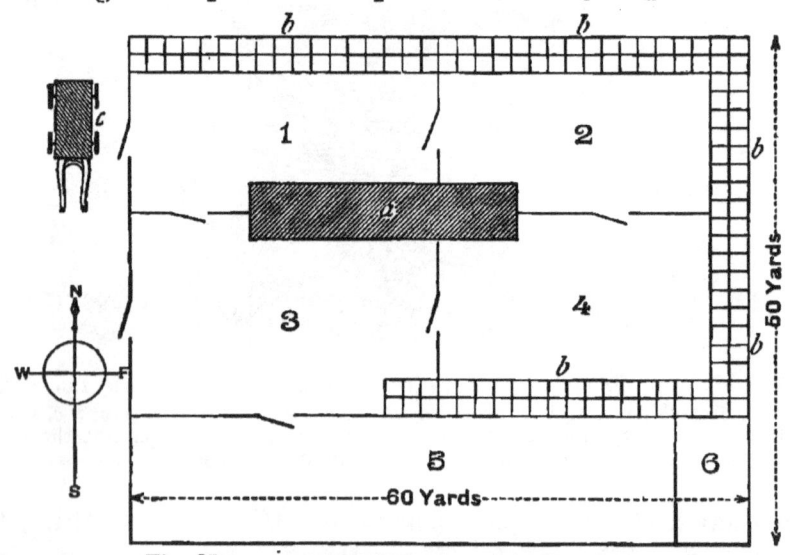

Fig. 38.—SHOWING PLAN OF A LAMBING PEN.

a, Straw rick; *b*, Coops, or cells; 1, 2, 3, 4, 5, Yards, well littered; *c*, Shepherd's van or hut on wheels; 6, Corner hurdled off for lambs to receive a little fine corn or cake in troughs.

The yards numbered 1 to 5 are employed for various sections of the flock. Ewes about to lamb may be brought into No. 3 at night, where they can be regularly looked to by the shepherd. Newly-lambed ewes will be placed in the cells, or coops, surrounding the enclosure. Twins and twin dams may, after an interval of two or three days, be placed in No. 1 yard; single lambs in No. 2; stronger lambs in No. 4; while No. 5 may also be used for older lambs and their dams, going out by day into turnips.

When the space becomes too crowded, a second, but simpler, pen may be erected in any convenient position, and the older ewes and lambs may be drafted there. A lambing pen is a most interesting sight, as hundreds of lambs are to be seen at various stages of growth. They play and race with one another around the enclosure, or retire into the hurdled-off space, where they are allowed a little corn or cake.

Young Lambs (January Lambing).

As soon as a lamb is born, it and its dam should be placed in a comfortable coop, and the shepherd should not lose sight of the young animal till he has seen it on its feet and sucking. The mother may have a little sweet hay, a mangel or turnip, and a little water, and if nothing goes wrong she will be able to go out into a littered yard after the third or fourth day. During the first week of a lamb's life it subsists entirely upon its mother's milk, but after that period it begins to try its teeth upon the finer portions of clover hay, turnip-tops, or to try the flavour of the dust of cake or of bruised corn. Where it is the intention to push lambs rapidly forward, they may at a fortnight old be encouraged to eat a little finely-crushed linseed-cake, malt, pease, or maize, placed for them in small lamb troughs in a corner, as shown in the plan of the lambing pen. The ewes also are gradually put upon cake or corn, with hay, roots, and water. The chief difference in management is in the amount of concentrated food given, as already pointed out. Lambs dropped in January and February are entirely dependent upon winter food, and such lambs are usually intended to be rapidly pushed forward.

At a fortnight or three weeks old they should be allowed to run forward beyond their mothers by means of the Lamb Creep, invented by Messrs. Carson and Toone. By this creep the lambs are able to run forward and to return easily to their dams, while the ewes are kept back in their own fold. Lamb troughs may be placed outside the fence, and suitable food placed in it for the young animals. The lambs can in this way crop the turnips and rape greens, and nibble the roots before the ewes, and thus are supplied with a variety of clean and fresh food.

The lambs are carried on upon this system until the middle or end of March, when the first green crop is ready, in the form of winter-sown rye. As the spring advances the choice of food increases, but there ought to be a supply of turnips and swedes to last well into May.

It is good policy to give lambs plenty of change, and at least two sorts of fresh, growing food every day. This is most easily expressed in the following way—the two foods being at no great distance from each other :—

Turnips, swedes, *and* rye.

Rye and ground swedes or mangel, *and* water-meadow.
Rye, with a few roots, *and* winter barley.
Winter barley, with a few roots, *and* trifolium.
Trifolium and ground-up mangel, *and* vetches.
Vetches, with ground mangel *and* rape.
Rape, clover, *and* cabbages.

This series of foods will last from March to August, and will be succeeded by a gradual introduction to winter feeding, in the form of early-sown turnips. By this time most of the lambs will have been sold, and the routine for another year's farming will have commenced. The amount of cake and corn given during the summer may vary, and be gradually increased from 2 oz. to 1 lb., or even more, and chopped hay (chaff) will be continued until spring keep is abundant.

Mangel, in small quantities, may also be given with advantage throughout the summer.

Young Lambs (March Lambing).

In many districts lambing does not become general until about the third week in March. When this is the case, the intention is to produce store lambs, and the keep is consequently less expensive, and the management simpler. The weather is milder, the days are longer, and the lambing is easier and safer. At this season of the year there is a fair amount of spring keep when the lambs are able to eat, and great dependence is placed upon grass, either in the form of permanent pasture or "seeds."

The general management of a ewe flock under such

circumstances is to lamb them down on grass, and draft the ewes as fast as they lamb on to the seed fields, where they get a few oats. Folding usually gives place to open-grazing, the ewes being run thinly over the grass fields, and shifted when the keep begins to run short. Whether the lambs receive any corn or cake entirely depends upon the ideas of the farmer, and many good flock-masters like to boast that their well-grown lambs have never tasted cake, as a proof of their hardihood and capacity for thriving.

Weaning does not take place until July, and after weaning the lambs again find their mothers, and follow them during the remainder of the summer.

The grazing is often poor and dry, and the flocks range over fells and high-lying pastures at small expense. The chief items of management in these cases consist in changing the sheep from pasture to pasture, and in guarding them against the attacks of flies and other mishaps. After the ewes are shorn the lambs are dipped, to kill the parasites which affect them, and they are quietly carried on until the time arrives for selling the lambs, or putting them on to turnips for fattening.

This, in few words, is a picture of the ordinary course often pursued where the more forcing and complicated method, first described, is but little known. The system is more followed in long-woolled flocks than by the keepers of Down sheep.

Hill Lambs.

The latest period for lambing ewes on hill farms in Scotland, and on the moors of the north of England, is April. The management is still simpler and more primitive. Lambing takes place on the open hills, and there is great loss among both lambs and ewes. The sheep seldom taste cake or corn, and subsist entirely by grazing. On these farms the wether lambs are sent on to turnips in the winter, and return to the hills in the spring; and the chilver or ewe type are wintered on the lower and more sheltered pastures with the assistance of hay and a few oats.

Fattening Sheep.

When ewes and lambs are supplied with cake and corn, roots, and hay, and the lambs fall in January, growing and fattening proceed together, and it is quite possible to sell the lambs to the butcher during July, August, and September. The breeders of Hampshire and Southdown sheep frequently follow this system, and are recouped by the rapid growth of the lambs, and the quick return which they yield. We have often known wether lambs sold in August at 60s., or even 70s. each; and when fat lambs are reared they may go off at the first-named figure in June.

A more ordinary plan is to carry the lambs on with less pressure or forcing, and to finish the fattening during the winter, selling out those that are fit for the butcher from January to April. Sometimes they are shorn, and then fattened out on grass during the succeeding summer, at about sixteen months old.

The fattening of sheep is done in the open air, upon the land, the animals being penned between hurdles or nets, which are regularly shifted over the field. This is called close folding, and is well suited for all light or medium dry soils. The treading of the sheep consolidates the land, while their droppings enrich it. Light lands are too open and loose for corn-growing, but after they have been close folded with sheep in winter, they plough up stiff and solid, and will grow corn crops well.

On the contrary, naturally stiff soils are not suitable for winter folding, because the treading of the sheep's feet puddles and "poaches" the land. Clay soils are already solid and close enough in texture, and will not bear sheep, or any kind of treading, in wet weather.

It will therefore be seen that the benefit of winter folding with sheep is confined to light soils, and not only so, but sheep will thrive well and fatten quickly upon a dry light-topped soil, while they suffer in health when closely penned upon a muddy clay field. Both land and sheep are injured on clay soils, while both land and sheep are benefited on light soils.

Great Economy of Sheep-Folding.

When sheep can be folded upon land with advantage, a great saving is effected in many ways. In the first place, the turnips or swedes are eaten where they grow, and all the expense of pulling, throwing into carts, heaping, and covering with straw is saved. Secondly, the land is evenly manured without the aid of the dung-cart: a saving which amounts in ordinary cases to about 7s. 6d. per acre Thirdly, there is nothing wasted, for even fragments of turnips, pieces of hay or straw, and particles of cake or corn which may be blown out of the troughs by wind, or pushed out by the sheep, are all preserved as manure on the land. Not a particle can be absolutely wasted. It is the same with the droppings of the sheep. There is no black stream of liquid manure to be seen oozing from a sheep-fold, such as is so often seen running out of cattle yards. All the waste of fertilising matter, about which so much has been said at various times, is avoided by sheep-folding, and the economy is, in point of fact, perfect. The price of mutton is higher than that of beef, and yet it does not appear that it is more expensive to manufacture. On the contrary, we are inclined to think that sheep are less expensively managed than cattle, so that the higher value of the mutton ought to appear in increased profits; and this it probably does, as sheep-farming has generally been found to be a profitable pursuit in all parts of the world.

Turnips for Sheep.

The turnip contains 90 per cent. of water, and has, therefore, been condemned as a staple article of food. It is true that the turnip contains too much water, but it is a food of which sheep are very fond, and the solid or dry matter which it does contain is exceedingly digestible and highly nourishing. The turnip contains a great deal of sugar and soluble or digestible cellulose. When they are grown upon good land, turnips are capable of fattening a sheep, but it is a much wiser plan to use them together with other kinds of foods. Hay, being dry, and also containing a good deal of indigestible fibre, which is useful in adding bulk to the food, is an excellent addition to turnips. So also is straw, in the form of straw-chaff, or chop, as it qualifies the watery character of the turnip. Concentrated foods, such as oil-cake, beans, peas, oats, etc., given in small quantity, help to bring up the quality of the food to the proper standard. Turnips and straw would not be rich enough for fattening a sheep, and hay is not always either sufficiently abundant or yet good enough for the purpose. A few ounces of linseed-cake or of beans adds the necessary richness to the food, and the animals readily fatten.

We look upon turnips as the staple food of a flock of sheep in winter, and the hay, cake, and corn as supplemental or additional foods, given to qualify the watery turnip, and to enrich the food generally.

The animal must be filled to satisfaction, and not limited to a certain allowance. One or other food must be given freely, or *ad libitum*, but the appetite can be checked by other foods. Thus, 1 lb. of cake will satisfy a sheep as much as 10 to 12 lbs. of turnips—that is, if a sheep would be capable of eating 30 lbs. of turnips in a day, he would only consume 18 to 20 lbs., with 1 lb. of oil-cake, and water, in addition.

It is a serious objection to turnips as a main food that they are cold. On a frosty morning the turnips are frozen, and when a sheep eats 30 lbs. of frozen turnips he is afterwards required to raise this food from 30° Fahr.—or even a lower temperature than that—to 98° Fahr., or to the natural heat of the sheep's body. This can only be done by an expenditure of force, as the animal heat is well known to be kept up by the consumption of fat.

Now, fattening is simply the *accumulation of fat in the body*, which cannot take place until all the wants of the creature have been supplied. It is clear that if

30 lbs. of turnips are to be raised from 30° to 98° Fahr., a good deal of heat or of fat must be required to do it. Such a system of feeding is therefore irrational or foolish, and properly open to objection. If sheep are house-fed they always eat less, and yet increase in weight quite as quickly as if fed in the open air. This is simply because the fat—which in the open air is used to keep up the heat of the body—is stored up when the animal is brought into a warmer air. In order to secure the storing up of the largest amount of fat in the animal body, it is necessary that the animal should eat plenty, and that it should not waste fat by being exposed to cold winds, or by being required to raise a large quantity of water through 70° Fahr.

Turnips must therefore be used with judgment; and the best system is to give such a quantity of dry food that the appetite of the animal is checked, and the quantity of turnips it eats is reduced—not by starving, but by satisfying the animal in other ways. The turnip should be given in just sufficient quantity to satisfy the thirst, and to make the sheep independent of water. And yet it is advisable that fattening sheep should have a supply of water by them, so that they may in all respects feel comfortable and contented.

The Food of fattening Sheep

should be of a nature to assist in the growth as well as the actual fattening of the animal. Sheep are almost always young, and growing in bone and muscle, as well as in fat, and hence it is a mistake to only give them oily or fatty foods.

This is the reason why *albuminoid* or *nitrogenous* foods are of value to them. We have already explained, in speaking of cattle feeding, that not only does the animal increase in weight, but there is also a constant waste, and necessary replacement or repair, of the body going on. This must be supplied by food. This waste, together with the keeping up of the nervous system or strength of the animal and the warmth of the body, has not improperly been called the "life-tax" upon the food. This tax is a heavy one. The heart must be supplied with the power to beat, and the lungs and all the organs of the body must be kept in full action. If only sufficient food were given to keep the animal alive and healthy, there would be no storing up of fat. You will at once see that it is only the extra food which pays the grazier. He might, by only giving sufficient food, derive no benefit from any increase in weight; but by liberal feeding he secures a profitable increase in the weight of the animal.

Beans, peas, oil-cake, hay, and turnips, given in proper proportions and in sufficient quantities, allow the animal to increase in weight and store up fat. The reader would do well to again look at the section upon cattle feeding (pages 38-48), and will then be better prepared to follow the practical directions for the fattening of sheep.

Practical Directions for the fattening of Sheep.

Bearing in mind the principles laid down in the previous sections, we are now in a position to give directions as to how sheep ought to be fattened. Store lambs are put on turnips, gradually, during September and October, and in November they are entirely on winter food.

MANAGEMENT OF SHEEP.

It is wise to change food for stock gradually. For example: instead of folding sheep at once on turnips, they should have a few thrown about on their pasture, or be allowed to be folded for a few hours only, every day, until they become accustomed to them. White turnips are the best for this purpose, and swedes should only be allowed after the animal has become well used to turnips.

When teggs have been gradually brought on to turnips and into the sheep-fold, they may have a $\frac{1}{4}$ lb. of cake and corn. We will not say which cake or corn, because so much depends upon the relative prices of different foods at the time. If a farmer happens to have a large quantity of oats, he will use them for his sheep. If cotton-cake or linseed-cake, maize or beans, happen to be cheap, he will probably make his selection more according to market price than by the actual chemical composition of these foods.

Hay, either long (or as it comes from the rick) or cut up by the chaff-cutter, will be given, and racks containing oat or peas straw may also be supplied.

The quantities will be as follows:—

For the first month (say October)—
    $\frac{1}{4}$ lb. of cake or corn, or mixed cake and corn;
    $\frac{1}{2}$ lb. of hay;
    Straw and turnips *ad libitum*.

November—
    $\frac{1}{2}$ lb. of cake or corn;
    $\frac{1}{2}$ lb. of hay;
    Straw and turnips *ad libitum*.

December—
    $\frac{3}{4}$ lb. of cake or corn;

¾ lb. of hay;
Straw and turnips *ad libitum*.

January—
1 lb. of cake or corn;
1 lb. of hay;
Straw and swedes *ad libitum*.

It will not be necessary to increase these quantities. Next, as to the

Method of Feeding.

Fattening sheep should receive hay the first thing on a winter's morning, as more comforting than cold turnips. After the hay, the troughs may be filled with cut turnips, and these they will eat with more relish after their dry food. At twelve o'clock they may have their cake and corn. At two o'clock they will again have their troughs filled with cut turnips. At four o'clock, or last thing, they will have another feed of hay in sufficient quantity to employ them until dark. Feeding will be therefore followed up from 7 A.M. to 4 P.M. in the order given, and sheep so treated will fatten quickly.

Cutting Turnips.

Teggs will break their own turnips up to February, at which time they begin to cast their lamb-teeth, and at this period they should have their turnips sliced or cut into finger-pieces by means of the Gardner's Turnip-cutter (Fig. 39). Fattening sheep always do better on cut turnips, but store sheep, such as ewes, or ewe teggs for stock, will be able to help themselves off the standing crop. Again, white turnips are much softer than swedes, and so

MANAGEMENT OF SHEEP.

long as teggs are on turnips the cutting may be dispensed with; but swedes must be cut, more especially as the sheep are not so well furnished with teeth at the period

Fig. 39.—SHEEP TURNIP-CUTTER.

when swedes are eaten. When it is intended to cut turnips into troughs they are pulled up and thrown into heaps, containing about one cart-load each, and covered with straw and earth, and the turnip-cutter is drawn up by the side of such heaps, and wheeled from heap to heap. The turnips are dressed or cleaned with a knife before they are ground up in the cutter.

CHAPTER VI.

VARIOUS EVENTS IN THE LIFE OF A SHEEP.

Birth.

Many lambs are lost at birth. Weakly lambs require particular attention, but strong lambs will stand a great deal of hardship. If a lamb is unable to stand and suck, it should be put down by the fire in a basket and hand-fed with a tea-spoon, with milk drawn from its mother. A tea-spoonful of gin is an excellent medicine for such a lamb, and it is surprising how often these attentions are repaid by a quick recovery. We do not think it necessary to enter at length upon the subject of *parturition*, or birth, but every shepherd ought to know how to assist both the mother and lamb through this critical period. It is an anxious time for both shepherds and masters, and valuable lives are often lost. Those who mean to follow the arduous life of shepherds must learn all these particulars in the field or from other sources, but we have sufficient to occupy us in these pages without entering upon such matters.

Castration

is performed on the male lambs which are not required for breeding. It is best done soon after birth, but sometimes it is postponed until later. The flesh of castrated animals is much more tender and better-flavoured than that of entire males, and the animals fatten more rapidly, and are quieter, and, in all respects, better for the operation.

Tailing

is generally performed at the same time as castration. The tail is cut off either close to the rump or at the third or fourth joint. It has been objected that this operation is unnecessary, and even cruel, but a little consideration will show that it is humane, and essential to the comfort of the sheep. In the natural state the wool cannot have been so long or so abundant as in the domesticated sheep; neither was it ever intended by nature that sheep should be folded on turnips upon ploughed or arable land. The tail of a sheep is weak and limp, and cannot be used to brush away flies. It is too thickly covered with wool for whisking about, like the tail of a cow or horse, and it becomes covered with dirt. Nothing, indeed, can be more miserable than a long-tailed sheep when flies are abundant, for they settle about the tail, and breed maggots. In the winter, when sheep are folded on turnips, the tail becomes wet and covered with knots of clay and dung; and this again is a discomfort to the animal; so that it is much better to inflict a momentary pang than to allow the animal to be miserable all its life.

Weaning

is best done when lambs are about fifteen weeks old Lambs born in January are weaned in May, when food is abundant, and March lambs are weaned in July. Weaning is effected by separating the lambs from their mothers, the lambs being left upon good keep, while the mothers are shifted to dry and poorer pastures. (*See* Management of Ewes.) When it is the custom to keep sheep between hurdles during the summer, weaning is most easily effected by simply shutting the lambs off from the ewes for longer and longer periods, until they learn to do without milk. The old custom of milking ewes and making ewe-milk cheese has almost died out. When, however, a ewe is distressed with her milk, the shepherd draws it off to relieve her.

Washing.

Sheep-washing is generally done in running water about ten days before shearing. The operation is simple, and consists in swimming the sheep through the stream and keeping them a few minutes in the water, during which time the backs and sides are well scrubbed. They are then allowed to land. The yelk, yolk, or grease which all fleeces contain, is a true potash soap, and assists to cleanse the wool. Tub-washing in cold water has been recommended, but scouring with soap and the use of hot water is not desirable for the wool. As a modification of the old-fashioned wash-pool, the following plan has been suggested, and may be easily followed, especially in the neighbourhood of a stream. Two tanks are provided, each capable of holding about five sheep. In the first tank the sheep are washed, and the water is allowed to become greasy—or rather, soapy—from the natural yelk of the wool. After a thorough washing in No. 1 tank, the sheep are plunged in No. 2 tank, which is well supplied with clean water. It would answer the same purpose to give them a swim in a clear stream after they had been well washed in the greasy water. It must be remembered that the term grease, or greasy, is misleading, and that the grease is really soapy in its nature. In Germany and Hungary it is the custom to save the water in which sheep have been washed, and to evaporate it to dryness, and recover a large amount of potash from it.

Dipping.

Sheep are usually dipped once a year. This is not washing, but is done as a preventive of *scab*, and as a means of destroying parasites, which infest the wool and live on the juices secreted from the skin of sheep. Dipping is also considered to improve the colour and growth of the wool. Most sheep dips contain arsenic, but there are also non-poisonous sheep dips, containing glycerine, carbolic acid, and tobacco juice. A dip may be composed of 2 lbs. of white arsenic, 2 lbs. of pearl-ash, 2 lbs. of sulphur, and 2 lbs. of soft soap. This is suspended in a bath of about 100 gallons of water, in which the sheep are dipped. It is scarcely advisable in these days for farmers to make their own dips, as many excellent compositions are now sold, some being non-poisonous, and others poisonous. Among these we may mention McDougall's (non-poisonous) carbolic and glycerine dips, Campbell's, Cooper's, Biggs', Watson's, and Laidlaw's, all of which are in extensive use. The operation of dipping requires three men, one on each side and one at the head. The sheep is allowed to remain a few seconds in the bath, and is then placed in a drainer, when the dipping material runs back again into the bath.

J

There are serious objections to the employment of arsenic or mercury in sheep dips, and McDougall Brothers have made a successful effort to introduce a non-poisonous dip, which instantly kills all ticks, lice, maggots, and scab. Two gallons (20 lbs.) of the dip are dissolved in 100 gallons of water to destroy scab, ticks, or lice, and four gallons (40 lbs.) are dissolved in 100 gallons of water to waterproof the fleeces as a protection against cold.

Shearing.

Few scenes are more cheerful than that of sheep-shearing. When large flocks are kept the work is undertaken by parties of about a dozen men, who quickly strip off the fleeces and pass on to another farm. They are a hearty, independent lot of fellows, and each member of the company will shear his thirty-five sheep a day. The clipping often takes place in one of the old-fashioned roomy barns for which the southern counties are famous, and the sheep are penned and caught for the shearers by one of the farmer's own men. The farmer also undertakes to wrap up the fleeces. Shearing is done with a pair of spring shears held with one hand, while the other hand and arm grasps the sheep. Great care is needed to avoid cutting the skin; and as slight wounds are sure to be made, a vessel containing Stockholm tar is placed within easy reach for application to the cut surface. Shearing heavy sheep is severe work, as anyone may learn who has not been accustomed to it. To handle struggling sheep on a hot day from morn to dewy eve, and turn them about, requires strength, activity, and skill, and is well worth the 3s. 6d. a score generally paid.

When sheep are shorn for market the fleece is taken off with great care, and the shear marks form regular and almost ornamental rings around the body, and a considerable amount of art is indulged in, as a kind of fancy shearing. The shearer leaves diamond or lozenge-shaped patterns on either leg or on the quarters and shoulders, which are supposed to "set off" the sheep as he appears before the buyer. A badly-shorn sheep is certainly a miserable-looking object, and there is little doubt that good shearing helps to secure a better price.

A man will hardly shear more than twenty fat sheep for the market in the course of a day. To avoid a charge of cruelty, it is advisable to provide jackets made of strong and warm rug. to put on clipped sheep sent to market in severe weather. It is well known that the flesh of clipped sheep, if chilled, suffers, so that both on account of humanity and to satisfy the buyer this clothing ought to be provided. It is retained after the sheep is sold, as there is no necessity for providing for the wants of another person's sheep. Ewes and stock sheep are shorn with less care.

The Home fashion is to shear in a line *with* the ribs; the Colonial is to clip *across* the ribs and in a line with the back-bone. This is much the more rapid style, and a Colonial clipper will strip the wool off one hundred sheep in a day, but the ordinary tally is fifty-five. In Austro-Hungary the shearing is done by women on benches, and is performed with scissors. One of the newest improvements is the Wolseley shearing machine, made on the principle of the horse-clipping machines, in which the teeth of the clipper form a horizontal comb or series of points, closely met by a correspondingly divided upper blade. The Wolseley clipper is worked with a small vertical engine, so that all the shearer has to do is to hold and turn his sheep and guide the machine. By these machines a sheep may be beautifully shorn in five minutes, much more perfectly than can be done in the ordinary way. The engine works a number of machines by means of a long shafting carrying pulleys or sheaves at intervals, which work the blades of the machines. The Wolseley Sheep-Shearing Machine Company estimates the advantages of its invention at 1s. 4d. per head, or 26s. 8d. per score of sheep, which is a very considerable saving. The average tally of one man with these machines is said to be 115 per day on Colonial sheep. A long tube hanging from the top revolves a flexible spindle, made to revolve rapidly by means of two cog-wheels. The other end of the spindle is attached to the clipping machine and causes the blades to work rapidly as the shearer guides them. The principle is the same as has been long applied by dentists for filing teeth in the mouths of their patients with a small rapidly revolving instrument only too well known to many of us. A similarly rapid motion is given to the blades of the shearing machine, and the wool rolls off the body of the sheep with great speed and perfect success.

A still later development is the "compressed air sheep shearer" brought out by the Australian Shearer Company. The clipper differs but little from the one just described, but it is actuated by compressed air instead of belting or gearing. This machine was first brought prominently into notice at the Show of the Royal Agricultural Society at Doncaster, 1891. The machine can be driven by hand, horse or water power, but better still by steam, gas, or kerosene engines.

Flies and Foot-rot

are two of the greatest troubles to sheep farmers. We shall not try to describe all the diseases to which sheep are liable as the subject is very vast, and could not be properly treated of in a small book like the present. Sheep are very difficult to "doctor." If a sheep is taken seriously ill it is only too likely that it will not recover. The most ordinary plan when a sheep takes ill is to kill it and sell the carcase for what it will fetch. It is true that this is not a course that can be approved of, because when an animal is ill its flesh is often unwholesome, although thorough cooking will generally render it harmless.

The natural feeling among farmers is not to allow an animal to die which may yet be slaughtered, and it is not likely that they will alter their practice. If a sheep is seen to "falter," or sicken, it is at once killed and the meat is sold at a reduced price, and so far as economy is concerned this is a better plan than to treat the animal with medicine.

The evils of flies and of lameness are, however, so constant that they may almost be said to give employment to shepherds throughout the year. Tending flocks often means a struggle against the flies and the foot-rot, and we shall therefore devote a little space to these two plagues.

FLIES attack the heads and tails of sheep. They seek out any spot where dirt or damp can be found, and tease the sheep by their bites and the trampling of their tiny feet, as well as by breeding maggots in the wool.

When flies once attack the head of a sheep they never let it alone. They swarm upon it and form what appears like a black cap on the poor creature's crown. They suck out the juices of the skin, and wear it away until they make a scald.

The unfortunate animal cannot rest or feed, and it is impossible for him to thrive. And yet the remedy is simple, for if a mixture of train oil and sulphur is prepared and a little of it be smeared over the sheep's head, not another fly will come near it.

When flies deposit their eggs on the tail, or elsewhere on the body of a sheep, the maggots quickly find their way to the skin and cause irritation and exudation. They produce in this way a scald, often extending over a large surface, and unless the sheep is looked to it may die from pain, much as though it had been burnt. McDougall's sheep-dip may be applied raw, or undiluted, by either pouring it over the wounded part or applying it with cotton wool. Mercury stone is very poisonous, but is commonly carried by shepherds, who rub it over the affected parts to destroy the maggots. In bad cases the wool comes off and disfigures the sheep. Flies are most troublesome in wet and warm weather, during the later summer and autumn.

FOOT-ROT—LAMENESS.—Sheep are often lame, but not always with true foot-rot. When their feet are neglected the hoof grows over the sole of the foot and bends over it, and gravel and hard clods of clay lodge between the overgrown hoof and sole causing lameness. In such cases all that is needed is to catch the sheep and with a sharp knife to pare the foot and restore it to a natural condition.

True *foot-rot* may be induced by neglect, where the conditions exist for its spread. It is, however, a contagious or catching disease, and often remains in the ground ready to break out.

It is a growth of a *fungoid* character, and burrows between the wall of the horn and the sensitive part of the foot. The horny part of the foot separates from the inner sensitive portion, and a spongy dark-coloured and corrosive substance, having an offensive smell, extends under the horn. The first thing necessary is to catch the sheep, and having set him on his rump on the ground, to cut away all the horn affected, and remove the fungous growth. This is done with care; and after the foot is thoroughly exposed and cleaned, an *astringent* is applied in the form of powdered blue vitriol, sulphate of zinc, butter of antimony, or some kind of foot-rot paste sold for the purpose. Such a lotion is the Australasian Foot-rot Lotion, sold by K. Sando and Co., Wool Exchange, Coleman Street, London.

In simple cases of foot-rot the sheep is treated as just described, and allowed to go free. Foot-rot is sometimes a very serious affair. It is always dreaded, as likely to prevent sheep from thriving, but if allowed to go too far the entire foot comes off, and the animal gradually pines away and dies.

Even in serious cases the treatment just described may be employed. After cutting away every part of the diseased horn, even although the whole foot is involved, the foot should then be washed in a solution of chloride of lime, in the proportion of one pound to one gallon of water. This will purify the surface, and prevent sloughing and mortification. The chloride or butter of antimony may then be applied with a feather to all the exposed parts of the foot. Youatt says—"There is no application comparable to this." It is a caustic which acts rapidly, but is not of a corrosive nature, and soon becomes diluted with the juices of the foot. Now wrap a little clean tow round the foot, and bind it tightly round with tape, and let the animal be placed on a dry pasture or in a clean and well-littered yard. The bandage should be opened every day, and the foot dressed. Any fresh appearance of the disease must be checked with the knife and touched with the caustic. The new horn must also be watched. If it is healthy, nothing need be done, but if it is soft and spongy the caustic must be applied.

Liver Rot.

Another dreadful disease to which sheep are liable is the "rot," or, more properly, the liver rot. So fearful is this disease that cases are common in which the entire flock has been swept away. The worst of rot is that an act of carelessness may easily cause it, and all the sheep which have been allowed to wander on to a piece of "unsound" ground are likely to suffer. To make our meaning more clear, it must be mentioned that any boggy, low-lying, spongy, or marshy ground may, at certain seasons of the year, cause rot. Many pastures are known to rot sheep, and cannot be stocked with them. The most fatal times of the year for sheep contracting the disease are late summer and autumn. In the spring of the year much land which is unsound at other parts of the year may be safely grazed. It is, for example, the custom to graze both ewes and lambs, as well as teggs, on water meadows in April and May, but it would not be safe to trust them on the same land in July and August. The cause of liver rot is the taking into the system, through the mouth, of a small shelled mollusc, known as the *Lymnius truncatulus*.

This small snail, it appears, contains a very minute *parasite* (entozoon), or what we may speak of as a worm for the sake of simplicity, which finds a suitable place for living and breeding in the bile ducts of the liver of sheep and cattle.

To cattle it does not do much harm, as the ducts are large. In the liver of the sheep, however, it proves fatal, for it completely chokes up the ducts, causes inflammation, deranges the entire liver, which becomes rotten, and, as a consequence, the sheep pines away and dies. It is curious to notice that in the earliest stage of this disease sheep fatten more rapidly, and so well is this known that butchers and graziers have been known to "coathe" or "rot" sheep which are intended to be slaughtered, so as to cause them to fatten more rapidly. When the first stage is over the animals become weak, and pine away until they die. The last serious outbreak of rot occurred after the wet season of 1879, and so widespread was the disease that the entire sheep-stock of the country was reduced by millions. The disease, after the first or thriving stage, shows itself first in the eye. The vessels in the corner of the eye become pale and yellow, and later the tongue and mucous membrane of the lips become tinged with yellow. The skin becomes spotted yellow and black, and the animal becomes spiritless. The wool comes off, and the animal wastes away, purges, and gradually becomes thinner and thinner, until death puts an end to its sufferings. When a rotten sheep is killed a yellow fluid is seen to extend over the whole body. The liver is completely rotten, and the ducts which carry the bile are found full of flukes, or little flat, oval-shaped worms.

There is no cure for rot, but it may be prevented by keeping sheep only upon sound ground. The effect of continued wet weather no doubt causes ground which is usually sound to become dangerous, but on the chalk hills and in other high-lying dry situations rot is never found.

It has also been often noticed that healthy sheep may contain a few liver flukes, but unless they are present in large numbers they do not affect the health of the animal.

Scab.

Reference has been made to scab under the head of "dipping." This is a skin disease of such a fearful character that it is a punishable offence to offer scabbed sheep upon the market. Sheep affected with scab rub themselves, and are affected with a constant itch. Sometimes the skin appears perfectly clean, but generally the scab appears more like what is known as mauge in other animals. The skin becomes rough, and a scurf forms at the bottom of the wool, near the skin.

Scab in sheep is caused by a minute *acarus* of irregular form. They are barely visible to the eye, but may be readily seen on a black surface. When magnified, they are seen to be of two sexes. If female *acari* are placed on the wool of a sound sheep, they quickly travel to the root of it, and bury themselves in the skin. There is then nothing more to be seen except a minute red point. On the tenth or twelfth day there is a little swelling, which may be detected with the finger. On the "sixteenth day the swelling or *pustule* breaks, and the mothers again appear with their little ones attached to their feet, and covered with a portion of the shell, from which they have just escaped. These little ones soon again penetrate the skin and begin to multiply, until the poor animal has myriads of them to prey on him and to torment him, and it is not wonderful that he should speedily sink" (Youatt).

The treatment of scab consists in dipping the sheep in a bath, which kills the *acarus*. The substances relied upon are arsenic, mercury, hellebore, and tobacco. Carbolic acid has of late years been found to be a cure for scab. It is carefully compounded in the McDougall dip. In the directions for using this remedy for scab, the shepherd is instructed to use two to four gallons of the dip to one hundred gallons of water, and to keep the animal immersed for one minute, while men remove the crusts from the scab spots as far as possible, so that the liquid may reach the "insects" under the crusts. If possible, keep the bath warm while dipping for scab, in order to soften the spots and allow the liquid to penetrate more freely. A repetition of this treatment will be found advisable.

As in other cases, prevention is better than cure, and sheep should be examined for scab before they are purchased. It is also wise to dip all newly-purchased sheep before allowing them to mix with the flock. The annual dipping of all sheep is no doubt a preventative against scab.

CHAPTER VII.

PIGS.

PIGS are not so important as farm stock as either cattle or sheep. Taking the total number of each of these animals in Great Britain, as returned by the Board of Agriculture, they were in 1890 as follows :—

Cattle	6,508,632
Sheep	27,272,459
Pigs	2,773,609

On all farms pigs are kept, but it is not uncommon to find only a few, and there is an impression that too many pigs are not desirable.

The pig, if less important as farm stock, is more generally appreciated among the general population. He is a favourite not only with the farmer, but with all classes of the community, from the highest to the lowest. No mansion would be complete in its offices without a well-contrived pig-stye for the accommodation of these thrifty animals. Every rectory or vicarage ought to possess, at convenient distance, a place for keeping a couple or more pigs. Every householder in the country, if possible, keeps a pig. Among establishments and trades, such as workhouses, asylums, hotels, inns, slaughter-houses, and many other places, the pig is ever ready to prevent waste, and to consume refuse food. Wherever there is a garden there ought to be a pig, and hence to the cottager, as well as to the farmer, the pig is an object of interest. He is the poor man's bank, a true thrift-box and save-all while alive, and after death a comfort so long as a vestige of him remains.

No animal is more completely useful and so free from offal. From his head is made brawn or collared head—a dish fit to set before a king. The whole of the carcase, tail and feet included, is excellent, either as pork, or cured. The Americans say with truth, but also with a touch of humour, that every part of the pig is useful except the "squeak." The bristles make brushes, the skin saddles, the intestines are used for packing meat in the form of savoury sausages, the bladder is filled with the lard which is made from the melted inside fat: so that from snout to tail the pig is excellent.

Origin of the Pig.

The domestic pig is derived from the wild boar, an animal which abounds in Germany, Russia, and Spain, and up to the time of Charles I. was found in our own forests.

The reader will remember that the ox and the sheep are not represented by any really wild animal which may be at once recognised as their ancestors. Naturalists are obliged to study forms now extinct before they can say, with any certainty, where our cattle came from, and as for sheep, we are almost in the dark as to the original form. But the pig may always be derived afresh from the wild boar. To speak more exactly, our improved races of swine are descended from two or three types of pig, all of which now exist. There is the wild boar of the European and Indian forests, known scientifically as the *Sus scrofa*. There is the Chinese, Malacca, Siamese, or Cambodian hog, which is found in a domesticated condition over vast regions in South-Eastern Asia; and, lastly, the South European or Neapolitan pig, found in Italy and other southern countries of Europe. These pigs have been crossed and blended together by breeders in order to produce various races of English pigs, all of which have their admirers.

The Wild Boar (*Sus scrofa, vel aper*).

This is a formidable wild animal, furnished with terrible weapons in the form of tusks, which he keeps sharp, and uses on slight provocation. He is so swift that he can keep up with a horse, and can climb the steepest hills with ease. He lives principally on roots, which he grubs up with his strong snout, but will also eat animals and carrion. He gives splendid sport to the hunter, as he is alert, cunning, and dangerous, and requires to be pursued with all the caution and dexterity which is dear to the sportsman. Professor Low writes as follows of the wild boar:—"There is something noble in the courage of this powerful and solitary creature. All his strength seems to be given for self-defence. He injures no one, unless when disturbed in his retreat, or in the search of food which his nature leads him to seek. He does not court a combat with enemies that thirst for his blood, but for the most part seeks to secure himself by betaking himself to the nearest covert. If attacked by savage dogs, he sullenly retreats, turning often upon them, and driving them back by his formidable tusks. When wearied and tormented, and forced at length to fight for his life, he turns on his persecutors, and aims at vengeance. If struck by the spear or ball of his pursuers, he has been known to disregard all other enemies, and single out his destroyer. When pursued by dogs, he rushes fiercely upon

Fig. 40.—WILD BOAR (*Sus scrofa*).

the foremost and strongest, maiming and killing numbers of the pack in an incredibly short time. In like manner he dashes at the foremost horseman, overthrowing the horse and his rider in a moment."

This fine creature abounded in our own country in the twelfth century, during the reign of Henry II., together with wolves, wild bulls, and other game in the great forests around London.

It is not easy to recognise in this noble denizen of the forest the indolent and greedy inhabitant of the pig-stye, and yet we are assured that the process of domestication and degradation is rapid. If the wild pigs be taken young from their mothers in the woods, they become nearly as docile as the domesticated races, and in a single generation all the fierceness which distinguished the parents is lost. We cannot do better than once more quote from the late Professor Low:—" When the wild hog is domesticated, these changes, amongst others, take place: the ears, not being required to collect distant sounds, become less movable; the formidable tusks of the male, no longer needed for self-defence, diminish; the muscles of the neck, not being exercised in the same degree as in the natural state, become less developed, and the head becomes more prone; the back and loins become longer, the body is rendered more capacious, and the limbs become shorter and less muscular; and anatomy shows that the stomach and intestinal canal have extended. . . The animal becomes diurnal in its habits and does not choose the night for its search after food." The female becomes more prolific, producing young both more often and in larger numbers. The animal becomes more greedy and less particular in the matter of food; it becomes naturally corpulent, and fattens readily. In the domesticated hog the number of teeth diminish, so that instead of six incisor or cutting (front) teeth in the upper, and as many in the lower jaw, found in the wild animal, he possesses only half that number. In countries where the pig has not been improved or carefully bred and crossed, the domestic pigs in many respects resemble the wild boars, as they are wild and grisly in appearance, but they never appear to regain the truly wild character. It is therefore clear that in the wild boar we find the ancestor of our own domesticated pig. As previously mentioned, the improved races have been crossed with other forms, among which the most important is the *Sus Indica,* or

"Chinese" Pig.

The kingdoms of Cambodia, Siam, Cochin-China, and Malacca are covered with magnificent forests, in which, among other animals, the wild hog abounds. The so-called Chinese pig, however, appears to have been domesticated for a longer period than our own native race, and it is doubtful if the parentage in the remote past has been the same as that now found in the native forests. There are several races of these pigs, differing in size and colour, but all of them are peculiar for their fattening properties.

The Chinese feed more largely upon pork than on any other animal food, and to this fact some persons have attributed the rejection by the Chinese of the Mohammedan faith, which forbids the flesh of swine. The Chinese are also said to use the milk of the sow as an article of food.

These pigs are found over a vast tract of territory, and are known by various names. The type most in favour in this country for crossing with our own native breeds is described as of small size, with a cylindrical body, hollow back, belly near the ground, short in the limbs, covered with soft bristles approaching the character of hair, colour black or rich copper colour, ears short and erect, head hollow or concave and short, arriving quickly at maturity, and fattening on a small quantity of food.

South European Pigs.

Hogs have been imported from Malta and Naples, and are known as Maltese and Neapolitan. They are black in colour, have very little hair, are long in the nose, and of rather small size. Some of the best Italian hogs are said to be found in the Duchy of Parma, and all have been introduced into this country, and have assisted to form our races.

ENGLISH BREEDS OF PIGS.—THE BLACK BREEDS.

1. The Berkshire Breed.

This breed is described by Professor Low as usually of a reddish-brown colour, and in his coloured illustration of

Fig. 41.—BERKSHIRE.

our domestic animals he gives as an example a red-coloured animal bred by Richard Astley, Esq., of Old-stone-hall, to represent the breed. The Berkshire pig of the present day is black, broken in certain places with white, and his turned-up nose is very different from the long nose shown in Professor Low's drawing. The breed has indeed been improved with Chinese crosses, and now is very unlike the drawing which represented him some fifty years ago. No race is more popular in the midland and southern counties, but in the north of England the white breeds are more in favour.

The Berkshire pig is of medium size, being inferior in this respect to the large Yorkshire breed. He may be described as follows :—The head is short, broad and hollow in the forehead, the nose being very much turned up. There is a streak or star of white on the forehead, which is characteristic of the breed; the feet, and often the tip of the tail, are also white. The ears are rather large, and should be carried forward, and be inclined to lop over the eyes and nose. The crest should overhang the forehead; the neck is strong and arched, as is also the back, which forms a gentle arch from crest, or poll, to tail. The ribs are well sprung, and the loin is wide and well covered. The quarters must not droop suddenly, but partake of the general curve of the body from end to end; the sides are somewhat flat and deep, the hams are well developed, and the gammon, or lower end of the ham, falls on and touches the hock joint; the belly is near the ground; the forequarters, or fore-hams and shoulders, are well developed, and the space behind the shoulder is well filled up; the skin is black, with a reddish blush below, and is well covered with an abundance of bristle, or coat. The breed may be used for pork or for curing, and is a great favourite at all bacon factories, and commands a high price per score.

2. The Essex Race

is also a black breed, but differs from the Berkshire in being entirely black in every part of the body, and is not thickly covered with bristle. The head is long and the nose flexible, probably through the use of Maltese or Neapolitan crosses. The Essex pig is flat or oval in carcase, and wants the width and solidity of the Berkshire pig. It is a remarkably quick and kind feeder, and produces flesh of particularly white and tender character. Its want of coat argues a delicacy, which might unfit this breed for roughing it in straw-yards in winter, as "coaty" pigs are always preferred for this purpose.

3. Other Black Races.

The black Suffolk, Dorset, and Hampshire pigs are also famous, but taking our great agricultural shows as our guide, we consider that all the remaining black races may be merged as larger and smaller black breeds, while the Berkshire and the Essex stand out prominently as definite races, requiring separate mention.

4. The Tamworth Race.

The Tamworth pig is of red colour. As the wild boar is of the same russet tint, and the old Berkshire, as figured by the late Professor Low, was also red, we see in this colour the remains of a hue which was probably more general at one time among pigs than it is now. That this was the case might easily be proved by quotations from writers upon live stock early in the present century. The author first saw a Tamworth pig in 1865, and was struck by its large size at an early age, and by its distinctive character. The quick growth of the breed was at that time well known and much spoken about. In 1879 Messrs. Harris, the great bacon curers at Calne, in Wiltshire, issued a circular calling attention to the "excessive fatness of bacon pigs, and recommending judges at shows to be guided by the weight of *flesh* carried on the most valuable parts." The reaction against fat meat which has taken place during recent years has brought forward the Tamworth breed, which appears to have been less affected by the Chinese crosses used on most of our breeds, and to have retained a greater power of developing muscle or lean meat. They are somewhat gaunt—"great high-backed, slab-sided creatures"—as Mr. G. M. Allander calls them, although himself an admirer and improver of the race.

THE WHITE BREEDS.
5. Large and Small Yorkshires.

We may even go a step further, and divide the Yorkshire breed into large, medium, and small, but the middle race is much less definite in its character. The large Yorkshire is an immense creature, rivalling a bullock in weight. He is of rosy rather than white colour, and the skin is covered with straight bristles. The head

Fig. 42.—SMALL YORKSHIRE.

is long and straight; and if he has a fault, it is that he is disposed to grow to too great a size. According to the old saying, "little pigs make the best of bacon," and certainly the large Yorkshire, although he is unquestionably little at one time of his life, cannot be spoken of as a little pig. The highest price per score is now given for pigs which, when slaughtered and dressed, weigh about one hundred and sixty pounds, or eight scores.

The small Yorkshire is at once known by his somewhat

smaller size, although they also may grow to a great weight. They are rounder or more cylindrical in form, are short in the head and turned up at the nose, and are well covered with a curly silky coat. These pigs are of better quality than the large breed, but give the impression that they are almost too highly improved. They are exceedingly short in the leg, and so sleepy that they often seem as if they could not be roused. These are the pigs which in show-yards are often seen reclining on wooden pillows, to keep their nostrils free of straw and litter, which might interfere with their breathing, and smother them. They are a valuable breed of pigs, but too much inclined to lay on fat rather than flesh. They might be spoken of, in the language once applied to our very fat breeds, as "bladders of animated lard." Still, we have no wish to run down the small Yorkshire pig, as he is an estimable creature, and has many admirers.

6. Other White Breeds.

The Yorkshire white breeds are by no means entirely confined to Yorkshire, neither are they of pure Yorkshire origin. The late Prince Consort was a great improver of pigs, and the Windsor breed is well known all over Europe as a first-class white race of pigs. There is also a breed which is known as the Coleshill, bred by a former Earl of Radnor, whose stock was dispersed in 1869, and was largely bought by the breeders of Yorkshire pigs. These were also known as White Berkshires. There is a rather coarser long-haired pig to be found in Herefordshire, and named after its county; and we may mention a small and fine pig, known as the White Suffolk.

CHAPTER VIII.

MANAGEMENT OF PIGS.

We shall not find it necessary to devote so much attention to the management of pigs as we have done to that of cattle or sheep.

The management of pigs is simpler, and it is also better understood by most people. It may be divided into breeding, rearing, and fattening, and one more branch may be profitably considered—namely, the curing of bacon, which we propose to treat of fully.

The Breeding of Pigs.

The pig is one of the most prolific of animals. We wonder if our readers have ever attempted to calculate the vast number of pigs which a sow is capable of producing through her female descendants in a period of six years. A sow ought to produce two litters a year of at least six each time, of which half may naturally be expected to be females. Each of these sows may, for the sake of calculation, be supposed capable of producing young at one year old, although in ordinary practice fourteen months would be a more usual age. These will also produce two litters of six each every year, half of which are females; but no sow must be kept for breeding after she is three years old. Here is a question in arithmetic which might be worth following out; and if it is done, the number of pigs produced in six years will be seen to be prodigious.

The calculation is made as follows: if we suppose our six years to commence with a sow one year old, just farrowed, we shall then have the following table, showing the produce in sows alone:—

Years.	No. of Sows.	No. of Suckers (females).	No. of six m'ths old hilts.
0	1	3	—
½	1	3	3
1	4	12	3
1½	7	21	12
2	19	57	21
2½	39	117	57
3	92	276	117
3½	202	606	276
4	459	1,377	606
4½	1,026	3,078	1,377
5	2,311	6,933	3,078
5½	5,187	15,561	6,933
6	11,661	33,983	15,561

The total number of female pigs, big and little, would in this case be 61,205, and as there would have been born an equal number of male pigs, the total descendants of the original sow would have numbered 122,410. In another six months this number would have risen to 257,534, and at the end of the seventh year to 600,120. With such a result we need not wonder that the price of pigs is quickly reduced when they become dear. Any scarcity of pigs is much more easily put right than is a scarcity of sheep or cattle, because they only produce young once a year, and generally one at a time, so that a regular increase in the number of females cannot be relied upon. The above calculation appears quite reasonable, because six is a small litter, and sows often produce twelve, and even as many as eighteen, young ones at a birth.

Sows.

From what has been already said, sows may produce young at a year old, but about fourteen or fifteen months old is more usual. A sow goes sixteen weeks in young, and generally suckles her young for eight weeks. If she breeds regularly, the year will be divided as follows:—

The first trip is farrowed about	February 1st.
Pigs weaned about................................	April 1st.
The second trip is farrowed	August 1st.
Pigs weaned about................................	October 1st.

Sows will continue to breed for several more years than we allowed in our calculation, but three years old is a good age to fatten them off; and if they are allowed to live much longer they become very unsaleable.

Sows must be allowed plenty of exercise and freedom. When they can roam in the pastures and get their own living, they are always more healthy, and likely to bring large and healthy litters. They should be, if possible, allowed a paddock, with a good supply of water and a hovel or hovels to retire into. A copse is also well suited for pigs, as they enjoy shade and a natural life. They enjoy a good wallow in a mud bath, but are not naturally uncleanly animals. The mud, no doubt, is, in the long run, cleansing to the skin, and allays that irritation which is caused by exposure to the sun or the attacks of flies.

Sows are best fed with grass, and will also enjoy cut clover, cut vetches, cabbage, mangel, turnips, and almost any kind of green food. Their drink may be water, but wash or swill, such as whey or dish-washings, is also much relished. A small quantity of pollards, of brewers' grains, and of bran may be added to the contents of the pig-tubs, but sows should not be over-fed, and are more profitable when fed upon the natural waste substances of the house and farm. We believe that sows managed as recommended will be healthy and profitable, and that nothing more is necessary to keep them in full health and vigour.

Farrowing.

As farrowing approaches sows should be removed to the farrowing pen. They must be kept quiet, and free from all disturbing noises. They have an unnatural inclination at times to eat their offspring, and this extraordinary taste is developed if they are disturbed or frightened. The farrowing house is composed of an inner pen and outer court, and should be roomy, warm, and well ventilated. It should be protected from the north, and open towards the south. The inner or covered portion should be at least eight feet long and ten feet broad, and the outer court may be eight feet long and twelve feet broad. The floor may be concrete or asphalte, and slope on all sides towards a drain. The sheds must be spouted, and the feeding troughs be placed under the south wall. The main pen must be furnished with a railing supported on posts about seven inches from the wall, and the same height above the floor, to prevent the sow from lying too close to the wall. Heavy sows often let themselves down by leaning against the wall and sliding their feet outwards, until they slip down, and in doing this little pigs are often squeezed to death. The farrowing pen should be somewhat scantily supplied with short litter, as young pigs are liable to get entangled in long straw, and may, at such a time, be smothered by an unwieldy mother. Sows show some anxiety to find a nest as their time approaches. They are seen carrying straw about in their mouths, and their paps also begin to fill with milk. The sow should now be put into the farrowing pen, and left as quiet as possible until she has produced her litter. A dose of from a quarter to half a pound of Epsom salts may then be administered by mixing it with her food, and a little sulphur is also wholesome. This is the best way of giving medicine to a sow, as they are awkward brutes to drench.

After the first week has passed the sow and pigs may be removed to a second pen, in which the outer court is railed off into two parts, so as to allow the little ones to eat a little milk, with fine "sharps" mixed in it. They must be kept clean and dry, or their tails will rot off. Young pigs may be weaned at eight weeks old. During the time the sow is suckling her young she should have a liberal diet of barley-meal, pollards, and a few beans.

Store Pigs.

Stores should be kept hardy. We recommend a strong rough pig with plenty of hair as most likely to thrive in a farmyard, and unless pig-breeding is a speciality, too large a number is not desirable.

Many farmers find it profitable to keep three or four good sows, and to sell the pigs as soon as they are worth twenty shillings each, which will be at from twelve to sixteen weeks old. The February or March litters may be carried on till harvest, when they go out to stubble, and are fattened off by Christmas, at weights varying from seven to ten scores. A pig, if well managed, will increase at the rate of about one score of twenty pounds every month. They live on whey, skim-milk, butter-milk, house-wash, grass, garden stuff, or cut green food during the summer, with a little pollards or barley-meal mixed in so as to form a thin wash. When whey is not available, brewers' grains make an excellent wash, especially when a small quantity of pollards, bran, and barley-meal are added, keeping the wash thin or watery.

Store pigs should be allowed plenty of room, and are better in yards than close pens. They should, as far as possible, live upon the produce of the farm. During the winter months store pigs are allowed to run in the yards with the fattening bullocks, where they are useful in eating up what the cattle might waste, and in routing up and mixing the manure. Nothing escapes them in their industrious search for food. At the barn door, under the cattle-troughs, watching for the litter brought from the cow-sheds and stables, completely hidden under the newly-thrashed straw, seeking for odd grains of corn—hardy and cunning, pertinacious and alert—are the store pigs.

Fatting Pigs.

The favourite weight for bacon pigs is now 160 pounds; and this they ought to make in eight months from birth.

To speak generally, the spring litters farrowed in February are fattened off before Christmas, and the August litters are ready the following March. At five months old the pigs may begin to receive forcing food; and experience has shown that barley is highly suitable for this purpose. The experiments on pig-feeding carried out by Sir John Lawes at Rothamsted showed that, after all, the cottager is right in using barley-meal for fattening his pig. The meal is mixed with water or with wash of some kind, and as the pig fattens the food is made thicker, until, in the later stages, it is of such a consistency as to form into balls. Plenty of barley-meal, regular attention, and a comfortably and not too roomy stye seem, then, all that is necessary to succeed—to which ought to be added a good sort of pig.

And yet we should like to say a little more about pig-fattening, as much has been written on the subject. Thus, Mr. Sanders Spencer recommends that pigs, "after they are about five months old, should be kept in a confined place, and fed on meal made from one-seventh wheat and two-sevenths each of barley, oats, and rye. This should be ground as fine as possible, and the best return will be obtained from it if it is fed to the pigs *dry*, another trough being put in the stye, in which is always to be found a supply of clean water or dairy refuse, either in the form of skim-milk, butter-milk, or whey. By the time the pig is seven months old it ought to weigh 150 to 170 lbs., when it will command the highest price in the market."

One of the most important points which require attention is the production of lean meat, or muscle. The difference between pigs in the amount of lean meat they produce is wonderful. In some cases the bacon seems to be entirely fat, and in other cases it is beautifully streaky and well mixed. Mr. Thomas Harris, the great bacon curer at Calne, in Wiltshire, has for some years given a *bonus* upon lean pigs. The excessively fat pig is therefore at a discount. Young pigs, being muscular, contain more lean than old ones, and as they are making muscle they can be so fed and treated as to develop it. Everyone knows that exercise and good food develop muscle; and the pig is no exception to this rule. An old sow will not develop much, but simply lay on fat, whereas a young growing pig may be so treated as to develop lean meat. It is also a mistake to prolong the fattening process to a later period than will satisfy the great bacon curers in the matter of fatness.

"The best kind of pig," writes Mr. Harris, "for bacon purposes is one with long deep body and hind quarters: thin in the neck, shoulders, and jowls, and with plenty of hair, weighing seven to eight and a-half scores dead weight." "The Tamworth pig is, I think, the one which gives most lean meat, being a long, thin-shouldered, deep-sided animal with plenty of hair (which is always a sign of leanness), hardy, and prolific. This sort, crossed with the Berkshire or large Yorkshire, with judicious feeding, I consider makes the nearest approach to a model side of bacon." Next as to the effect of food. Mr. F. J. Lloyd says that a nutritive ratio (*see* page 41) of one to five is well calculated to produce *fleshy* animals—*i.e.*, animals containing much lean meat. This is true, and points clearly to the use of such foods as bean-meal, as well as barley-meal. Young animals always require foods rich in albuminoids, simply because they are making muscle, and by encouraging this tendency we secure lean meat. Such a diet as is recommended by Mr. Alexander Watt, in his Prize Essay on Dairy Farming in Devonshire, is well worthy of attention.

It consists of equal quantities of beans, maize, barley, and wheat-meals. This is no doubt better than pure barley-meal, because the nutritive ratio of barley-meal is 1 to 8, which is too low, and too much adapted for laying on fat. Skim-milk and barley-meal is also an excellent union of foods, because the nutritive ratio in skim-milk is very high, being 1 to 18, and when given judiciously with barley-meal it produces the necessary material for making muscle or lean. Once more, it is well to repeat that young growing animals will always be more likely to make lean than old animals which have done growing.

Bacon Curing.

We will describe the simplest method first, and then mention some plans for producing special or finely-flavoured hams. Bacon curing is a very simple operation, only requiring salt, and a little saltpetre for giving the required colour to the flesh.

Every householder should know how to cure bacon. Like baking and brewing, it is now carried out in large establishments, such as are to be seen at Calne, in Wiltshire, at Limerick, and on a still larger scale at Chicago, in the United States of America. In some of these bacon factories thousands of pigs are slaughtered every week, and the work is carried out on an extensive scale with the aid of machinery. In one of these factories at Limerick large and airy sheds, covered with light roofing, occupy a vast space. The pigs are killed by hoisting them up by one hind leg, and by means of a hook fitting into an overhead rail or bar, they slide down a slight incline to the "sticker," who, armed with a sharp knife, skilfully slaughters them as they pass him. The animal speedily bleeds to death, for the art of pig-sticking is well understood by the operator, and the carcase travels by its own weight onwards on the overhead rail until it is suspended over an immense tank of boiling water. In this it is plunged, and, floating through it, is fished up on the other side with wonderful speed, and lowered down upon an iron cradle, which is then passed for a few moments into a fiery furnace in order to singe it. The carcase is then slid on to another overhead rail, and is pushed on to be washed by means of jets of water which spout out of an iron casing so as to completely cover every part of the body. The next operation is scraping, and the washed and scraped pig is again pushed on to join a long rank of freshly slaughtered carcases, where it is opened, the viscera removed, the carcase cut down the back, and left to cool. We need not follow these operations in detail, but may say that when cool the carcase is cut down into sides, or flitches, and, in many cases, slid down a shoot into the cellars, where a man stands to receive them. They are then stacked up, one on the other, with the skin side downwards, each side being well covered with a mixture of salt and saltpetre. The thicker parts and hams are injected with brine by means of a force-pump, and the sides are left for a week. They are then re-stacked and fresh salted, and in a fortnight are ready for smoking. The whole process occupies three weeks, and the flitches are then packed and despatched to the bacon factors. We take the following more detailed description from Morton's "Cyclopædia":—

"The carcase of the hog, after hanging over-night to cool, is laid on a strong bench or stool, and the head is separated from the body at the neck, close behind the ears. The fat, and also the internal fat, are removed. The carcase is next divided into two sides in the following manner: The ribs are divided about an inch from the spine on each side, and the spine, with the ends of the ribs attached, together with the internal flesh between it and the kidneys, and also the flesh above it, throughout the whole length of the sides, are removed. The portion of the carcase thus cut is in the form of a wedge—the breadth of the interior consisting of the breadth of the spine, and about an inch of the ribs on each side, being diminished to about half an inch at the exterior, or skin along the back.

"The breast bone, and also the first anterior rib, are also dissected from the side. Sometimes the whole of the ribs are removed, but this, for reasons afterwards to be noted, is a very bad practice. When the hams are cured separately from the side—which is generally the case—they are cut out so as to include the hock bone, in a similar mode to the London mode of cutting a haunch of mutton. The carcase of the hog thus cut up is ready for being salted, which process in large curing establishments is usually as follows: The skin side of the pork is rubbed over with a mixture of fifty parts by weight of salt and one part of saltpetre in powder, and the inside parts of the ham, or flitch, and the inside of the flitch covered with the same. The salted bacon, in pairs of flitches, with the insides to each other, is piled, one pair of flitches above another, on benches slightly inclined, and furnished with spouts or troughs to convey the brine to receivers in the floor of the salting house, to be afterwards used for pickling pork for Navy purposes. In this state the bacon remains a fortnight, which is sufficient for flitches cut from hogs of a carcase weight of less than fifteen stone (fourteen pounds to the stone). Flitches of a large size, at the expiration of the time, are wiped dry, and reversed in their place in the pile, having at the same time about half the first quantity of fresh dry common salt sprinkled over the inside and incised parts, after which they remain on the benches for another week. Hams, being thicker than flitches, will require, when less than twenty pounds weight, three weeks, and when above that weight four weeks, to remain under the above-described process.

"The next and last process in the preparation of bacon and hams previous to being sent to market is drying. This is effected by hanging the flitches and hams for two or three weeks in a room heated by stoves, as in a smoke-house, in which they are exposed for the same length of time to the smoke arising from the slow combustion of the sawdust of oak or other hard wood. The latter mode of completing the curing process has some advantage over the other, as by it the meat is subject to the action of creosote, a volatile oil, produced by the combustion of the sawdust, which is powerfully antiseptic; the process also furnishing a thin covering of a resinous varnish, excludes the air, not only from the meat, but also from the fat, thus effectually preventing the meat from becoming rusted; and the principal reasons for condemning the practice of removing the ribs from the flitches of pork are that by so doing the meat becomes unpleasantly hard and pungent in the process of salting, and by being more exposed to the action of the air, becomes sooner and more extensively rusted. Notwithstanding its superior efficacy in completing the process of curing, the flavour which smoke-drying imparts to meat is disliked by many persons, and it is therefore by no means the most general mode of drying adopted by mercantile curers. A very superior variety of *pyroligneous* acid, or vinegar made from the destructive distillation of wood, is sometimes used on account of the highly preservative power of the creosote which it contains, and also to impart the smoked flavour, in which latter object, however, the coarse flavour of tar is given rather than that derived from the smoke from combustion of wood. A considerable portion of the bacon and hams salted in Ireland is exported from that country packed among salt in bales immediately from the salting process, without having been in any degree dried. In the process of salting above described pork loses from eight to ten per cent. of its weight, according to the size and quality of the meat, and a further diminution of weight, to the extent of five to six per cent., takes place in drying during the first fortnight after being taken out of salt, so that the total loss of weight occasioned by the preparation of bacon and hams in a proper state for market is not less, on an average, than fifteen per cent. on the weight of the fresh pork."

Wiltshire Bacon.

Pound and well mix for each pig a pound and a half of coarse sugar, a pound and a half of bay-salt, six ounces of saltpetre, and one pound of common salt. First sprinkle each flitch with common salt, and let the liquid drain away for twenty-four hours. Then take the above ingredients and rub it well into the meat, which should be turned every day for a month. Then hang it to dry, and afterwards smoke it over a wood fire for ten days.

Curing Hams.

Rub two hams with common salt, and leave them in a large pan for three days. Throw away the brine which has been extracted from the hams. Mix one pound of moist sugar, one pound of common salt, and two ounces of saltpetre. Well rub the hams, and place them in a suitable vessel, taking care that they are well covered with the salt. After three days pour over one quart of good vinegar. Turn daily in the brine for a month, and then take them out and rub them with bran. If thought desirable, they can be then smoked over a wood fire.

Sweet Hams.

Rub two hams with salt, and after twenty-four hours drain away the brine. Take a saucepan, and boil together three pounds of common salt, three pounds of coarse sugar, one pound of bay-salt, and three quarts of strong beer. Let the mixture boil for a quarter of an hour, and pour it over the hams, and let them remain one month in the pickle. Rub and turn daily under the pickle, and take out and smoke for one month over wood fire.

CHAPTER IX.
HORSES.

ENGLAND is as famous for horses as she is for cattle, sheep, and pigs. From the thorough-bred or race-horse to the cart-horse, she stands foremost among nations in this respect. The reader may wonder whether our English horses are superior to the beautiful horses of Arabia, which have so often been spoken of and praised, or the horses of Barbary, or the celebrated Turcoman horse. We believe they are. All of these horses have been used in forming the English thorough-bred, and it is not too much to say that for speed, endurance, and beauty the English horse excels them all. Other nations, being well aware of the superiority of English horses, are constant buyers, and give long prices to secure the best of our breeding animals, and a time may come in which we shall find ourselves beaten. There is no doubt that the competition is very keen and very close. We have, however, two strong points, one of which cannot be taken from us: and that is our climate. Much has been said against our variable and uncertain climate, but we should value it highly on account of its being suitable for all kinds of domesticated animals. If there is a climate more suitable for horses than that of England, it is to be found in Ireland. The virtue of our climate seems to be that it is temperate, and moist enough to cause an abundant growth of grass. The soil of Ireland mostly rests upon limestone, and thus is able to supply the material in sufficient quantities from which bone is made. Her pastures are particularly rich, which has earned for her the name of the " Emerald " Isle, and Irishmen are fearless riders and true lovers of the horse.

Our other safeguard is the natural love of animals, and the genius for breeding them which characterises our nation.

The Origin of the Horse.

We have stated that no true wild horse exists in the world, and need not now repeat the reasons for this opinion. The horse appears to have been domesticated so long since that the actual parent form has disappeared, and the so-called wild horses are considered to be the descendants of domesticated horses which have recovered their freedom. He is thus, in some respects, an artificial creature, and his form appears to have become moulded to the requirements of man in a very special manner.

The Book of Job is considered to be of great antiquity, and yet the description of the war-horse there given is the most spirited ever penned. The words occur in God's own rebuke to the patriarch, and may be here quoted as showing how perfect the animal was known to be, even in those far-off times. " Hast thou given the horse strength? hast thou clothed his neck with thunder? Canst thou make him afraid as a grasshopper? the glory of his nostrils is terrible. He paweth in the valley, and rejoiceth in his strength: he goeth on to meet the armed men. He mocketh at fear, and is not affrighted: neither turneth he back from the sword. The quiver rattleth against him, the glittering spear and shield. He swalloweth the ground with fierceness and rage: neither believeth he that it is the sound of the trumpet. He saith among the trumpets, Ha, ha; and he smelleth the battle afar off, the thunder of the captains, and the shouting." No one who has watched or bestrode a high-mettled steed but will feel the truth of this wonderful description. The horse, though timid when brought into positions new to him, is courageous when he knows what is expected of him. He is nobly excitable, and in war or in the chase he rushes on with such impetuosity that he is difficult to hold back. Especially in company with men and horses he "paweth and rejoiceth in his strength." The charge of cavalry is terrible and overwhelming, and has often turned the fortunes of battle. The Book of Job is thought to have been written about 1,500 years before Christ, and therefore indicates the great length of time that the horse has been domesticated. As, however, some scholars in these critical days consider that the Book of Job may not be so old as just stated, we will quote one more Scriptural authority which is of unquestioned and remote antiquity— namely, the song of Miriam, sister of Moses, who celebrated the overthrow of Pharaoh in the Red Sea in the words, "the horse and his rider hath He thrown into the sea"; and we read in Moses' own account that "the Egyptians pursued, and went in after them to the midst of the sea, even all Pharaoh's horses, his chariots, and his horsemen."

The Egyptians, therefore, had horses; but if we turn to the history of the twelve patriarchs going down to buy corn in Egypt, we shall find that they took asses with them, and no mention is made of horses until Egypt is reached. The Ishmaelites who carried Joseph into Egypt were mounted on camels, and there is no mention made of horses as existing among the patriarchs, but they possessed sheep, oxen, camels, and asses.

Although the descendants of Jacob lived four hundred years in Egypt, they do not appear to have acquired property in horses, and, indeed, were enjoined not to possess themselves of them. In their wars it was their custom to hough or hamstring the horses which they captured from their enemies. David hamstrung six hundred horses, and speaks with a sort of disdain of horses as an instrument of war, when he says, "some trust in chariots, and some in horses." The ass and the ox were the animals of burden or of draught employed by the Jews, and Saul, it will be remembered, was in quest of his father's asses, which had strayed, when he was called to be king over Israel. David, however, when he houghed six hundred horses, reserved one hundred, and Solomon broke through the customs and laws which had guided his predecessors, and formed a numerous body of horses and chariots, and established a trade in horses with Africa.

Arabia was not apparently possessed of horses at that time. Strabo, who wrote in the time of Tiberius Cæsar, states that neither Arabia-Felix nor Deserta possessed either horses or mules, but at and after the time of Mahomet the Arabs became horsemen. If, then, Arabia was destitute of horses, and Solomon imported from Egypt and other countries of Africa, we may infer that the Egyptian horses were of African origin.

The African Horse.

The African horse appears to be distinct from that of

Asia, and the most characteristic type is found in Nubia and the adjoining deserts. How far this remarkable race of horses extends into the burning regions of the interior we are ignorant, but the horses of Africa with which we are most familiar in Europe are those which inhabit the countries north of the desert of Sahara. They are termed Barbs, and they inhabit the kingdoms of Fez, Morocco, and all the countries eastward, to the deserts bordering on Egypt.

The Asiatic Horse.

This horse, although of a stronger and robuster type, has also been since the earliest times domesticated in the countries bordering on the Caspian and Euxine Seas, and is found in perfection near the Caucasus, in Armenia, and other parts of Asia Minor. The Circassians are famous for the beauty of their horses. The Turcomans and Kurds possess horses of great strength and power, and it was from these countries that the Turks derived their splendid cavalry with which they well-nigh subdued Europe.

Armenia, at an earlier period, supplied the merchant princes of Tyre and Sidon with horses and mules, and Homer, a thousand years before the Christian era, speaks of the horses of the same countries as yoked to the chariots of his heroes.

The Arabian Horse.

Arabia does not appear to have acquired the horse until the age of Mahomet. The Arabian horses are connected in all their characters with those of the Caucasus and Asia Minor; but inhabiting a very dry and arid country, they are smaller, but at the same time more compact, rounder in body, shorter in limb, with more bone and sinew than the Asiatic horse previously described. They are not often more than fourteen hands, or fifty-six inches, high. They are lean, slender, and somewhat narrow-chested, and are swift, agile, spirited, and gentle. They are by no means the fiery animals some people imagine them to be, but are docile and affectionate. These horses are produced in the largest numbers in the countries bordering on Syria and the river Euphrates, where the climate is temperate and food abundant; and south of the countries stretching from Mecca to the Persian Gulf they are few in numbers and stunted in growth.

Very fine horses are to be found in Persia, especially near the Caspian Sea. The Indian horses are small and inferior in temper to those of Arabia. In China the horse is not much esteemed, but in Tartary and Thibet they are numerous. The horses of the Kalmuks and those of Independent Tartary, owned by the Turcomans and others, have always been famous, especially for purposes of war. The region of Siberia contains herds of wild horses, but, as already stated, it is more than doubtful if these are truly wild, and they are now looked upon as having escaped from a state of domestication, and become wild in their habits. In Siam, Cambodia, and Malacca the horse is of pony size, fiery, tolerably swift, but not possessed of great powers of endurance. The inhabitants of these countries have never been horsemen.

The Wild Horses of South America.

That the horse is capable of regaining his freedom, and

of assuming once more the habits of a wild animal, is clearly shown in South America. It is well known that the horse did not exist in the vast new continent discovered by Columbus. It was imported by the Spanish soldiers of Pizarro and his compeers, and there multiplied with wonderful rapidity. According to Azara, when Buenos Ayres was abandoned, about the year 1535, its inhabitants left behind them five horses and seven mares, which had been brought from Andalusia. These soon multiplied, and gave origin to those vast herds which covered the broad plains southward and westward of the Rio de la Plata, while others, escaping from the settlement north of the same river, multiplied in Paraguay and other parts of the interior. Mexican horses have also escaped into the woods and savannahs, and become wild, and have extended northward to the Rockies and Columbia in the fifty-second and fifty-third parallels of latitude. The "wild" horses of the Falkland Islands furnish also another instance of how rapidly horses return to a state of freedom.

Darwin's Views as to the Origin of the Horse.

The great naturalist, Charles Darwin, was strongly of the opinion already given, that the horse does not now exist in the original form from which he was derived. He came to the conclusion that the horse is descended from an extinct stock which probably resembled the quagga, or in a less degree the zebra—that is, a more or less striped animal. He was led to this conclusion by noticing that in many parts of the world horses which have not been carefully bred, or which have continued unimproved, are furnished with a dark-coloured stripe, extending from the mane to the tail, like that seen upon the ass. Further, he noticed that in many cases the spinal stripe is accompanied by distinct shoulder stripes, and in others with cross-bars or markings on the hocks and inside the fore-legs. In rarer cases other markings similar to those found upon Burchell's zebra were observed, and from these and other observations he came to the conclusion that there is a tendency for horses to throw stripes. The appearance of these markings in horses bred in all parts of the world seems to indicate a lost character which now and then appears in the domesticated horse, which, it is therefore thought, is derived from a remote parent form of striped character, now extinct.

Older writers, such as the late Professor Low, to whose writings we are largely indebted for much information on horses, do not seem to have had any doubt as to the existence of truly wild horses in Asia and Africa. The light of science has, however, caused us to modify this view. The presence of wild horses in America and the Falkland Islands shows how readily the horse may become emancipated or free, and it is therefore exceedingly probable that the so-called wild horses of Siberia and Central Asia may also be the descendants of escaped horses.

English Horses.

When Julius Cæsar invaded Britain, in the year 55 B.C., he found the Belgæ possessed of horses, which they attached to chariots for the purposes of attack and defence. Whatever was the character of these early horses with respect to their size, strength, and proportions, it is probable that for many ages they underwent little change. The horses of Saxon England, for all we know, were much the same in character with the horses which encountered the Roman legions under Julius Cæsar. The Normans were, however, ardent admirers of the horse, and soon after their occupation arose the age of chivalry. The Norman knights are known to have imported the great Black horse of Flanders, as capable of supporting the weight of armour required in the warfare of those rude times. The Crusades brought our armies into contact with the superior Turkish horses used by the Saracens, and by degrees horses from Spain and Italy, Barbary and the Levant, found their way to the land of the Anglo-Normans. King John devoted his attention to the improvement of the native horses, and at one time imported one hundred stallions from Flanders. Edward II. imported horses from Lombardy, and Edward III. devoted a large sum to the purchase of Spanish horses. Henry VII. was the last of the English kings who maintained the usages of chivalry, and imported finer horses from Turkey, Naples, and Spain for the improvement of the royal stud. Owing, in a great measure, to the use of heavy armour, the English horses of this time appear to have been rather of the cart-horse type, even when employed for the chase. During the reign of Elizabeth heavy armour went out of use, and her successor, James I., favoured a sport which has had a great influence on our horses: namely, the horse-race. This idea was further encouraged, and became established as a national sport, by Charles II., and from this period a vast amount of care has been bestowed on horses devoted to the course.

The horses imported for this purpose were chiefly from Africa, from Asiatic Turkey, and, ultimately, from Arabia. The Barbs came generally from Morocco and Fez, the Turks from Smyrna, and the Arabs from the deserts adjoining Syria. From the reign of King James II. to Queen Anne the imported horses were Barbs and Turks, but chiefly Barbs, which had, therefore, the largest share in forming the character of the English race-horse. The pure Arabs were chiefly imported in the early part of the last century.

As the horses produced by crossing these various types with our native breed were constantly tested on the race-course, and as success on the turf is generally hereditary, it was natural that pedigrees should be carefully kept, and in this way the foundation was laid of what is now known as the English Thorough-bred horse. The various elements became fused together, with a magnificent result; and it is not too much to say that the English Blood-horse is unequalled in the world for strength, swiftness, and endurance. Although originally compounded of various races, his properties have now been transmitted through so many generations that he is properly regarded as pure-bred or thorough-bred, and in this peculiarity he stands almost alone.

The Thorough-bred is, in the first place, a racer, but his splendid qualities have been utilised for improving the standard of the inferior horses of the country. Thus, we find a large number of "half-bred" horses, by which term is meant any high-class horse which is not a pure-bred. Half-bred horses produced by the union of, it may be, cart mares, or mares of higher breeding, with a thorough-bred horse, give fine carriage-horses, hunters, and hacks or roadsters. In some cases they are nearly thorough-bred, while in others they are of less pure descent, and of heavier build. Horses are required for such a vast number of purposes that all degrees of size and weight find a market, but for all the classes of lighter or faster work "a dash of blood" is now thought to be essential. Thus, horses are needed for heavy broughams, wagonettes, dog-carts, trade vans, as well as for ordinary saddle purposes and the hunting-field; and the Thorough-bred lies at the foundation of all of these, though in a greater or less degree.

Fox-hunting, scarcely less than racing, has proved to be a great stimulus to the breeding of weight-carrying horses gifted with staying powers. It is therefore clear that the history of the English Thorough-bred is bound up with the general progress of breeding for the supply of all the better class of horses. (*See* Hackney Horses.)

English Cart-horses.

The origin of the English Cart-horse dates back to the time previous to the importation of those higher classes of animals which gradually produced the English Thorough-bred. At the time of Queen Elizabeth the coarse cart-horse form was the prevailing one, as may be seen from the pictures of the time.

We cannot, however, look upon English Cart-horses as all of the same general form. We have several well-defined races of draught horses, each of which is now bred with great care, and, although the term thorough-bred has been appropriated to the blood-horse, or racer, many of our

Fig. 43.—SHIRE HORSE, "SAMSON THE SECOND". (Property of the Earl of Ellesmere).

draught horses may well be spoken of as pure or thorough in their pedigrees.

The Old English Black Horse.

This breed is now better known as the Shire horse, which is the direct descendant of the Old English and European Black horse—one of the grandest and most widely extended breeds of horses. In the reign of Henry VIII. a law was passed that all stallions below a certain size (fifteen hands) should be confiscated, and that any mares not likely to breed foals of a reasonable size should, at the discretion of the drivers of the commons, be killed and buried. Professor Low speaks of these "monstrous edicts" as causing such a decline in the number of horses in England that Queen Elizabeth could only muster 3,000 cavalry when the terrible Spanish Armada threatened her kingdom with destruction. Mr. Walter Gilbey, who is a great breeder of Shire horses, takes a different view: namely, that "this statute no doubt served to build up what has since come to be called the *Shire* horse."

It is well known that from the earliest times a large and heavy race of horses of black colour existed in Europe. It was well known to the Romans, who derived the most powerful horses for their cavalry from Belgic Gaul. In the Middle Ages these horses carried knights and men-at-arms, and they are still used for mounting heavy cavalry throughout Europe.

The same widely spread race has long existed in England, under the name of the Old English Black horse. It has long been known, from the Humber, through the fens of Lincolnshire and Cambridgeshire, and extending westward through the counties of Huntingdon, Northampton, Leicester, Nottingham, Derby, Warwick, and Stafford, to the Severn. Other counties might be named north and south of those already mentioned, and hence the appropriate name of the Shire horse, or horse of the English shires.

It is the largest, heaviest, and perhaps grandest, horse in the world. At two and a half years old colts are often seventeen hands high, and, when weight is required, the larger descriptions of Shire horses are in most demand.

Three varieties of this race have been described: (1) The largest and heaviest kind, which is used for dray and railway work; (2) Waggon-horses; (3) Lighter horses, used for certain Household Cavalry regiments and for the melancholy task of drawing hearses and mourning-coaches. What is known now specially as the Shire horse represents an improved form of the heaviest and largest description of Black horses.

Professor Low, whose works on live stock were written some fifty years ago, relates that the unimproved, or original, type of Black horse had in his turn almost ceased to exist, but that "individuals are still to be met with, bordering on the commons or in possession of very old farmers." They had coarse heads, large ears, and thick lips largely garnished with hair, coarse shoulders, stout, hairy limbs, broad hoofs, and upright pasterns. Robert Bakewell, of Dishley, who has been already mentioned in connection with Longhorn cattle and Leicester sheep, was the first notable improver of the Old English Black horse. He went to Holland, and bought mares, which he crossed with the native stallions, and afterwards pursued a course of careful selection, with most excellent results. During recent years the type has been further improved, especially in the legs and pasterns, and are largely exported to America, where they are very popular. The Shire Horse Society and "Stud Book," and an influential list of famous breeders, attest the popularity of this famous breed.

The Clydesdale Horse.

This breed occupies a similar position in the lowlands of Scotland and border counties to that of the Black or Shire horse of the English midlands. In appearance they are similar; and when we remember the wide distribution of the European Black horse, and the fact that a Duke of Hamilton crossed the mares of his country with Flemish stallions, it is more than probable that the two races are closely related. The Clydesdale horse is of the larger class of draught horses, the ordinary height being sixteen hands. They are often black in colour, but may be brown, bay, and even grey. They are longer in body than the Old English Black horse, and less weighty and compact, with a quicker action. For farm work they are superior to the English breed, as they step out more briskly, and are less heavy upon the land. They find their favourite home in Lanarkshire, and are largely found in Renfrew, Ayr, and Dumfries. These horses are also much sought after by American buyers, and high prices are given for them. As an example of the value of these horses, we may mention that the late Mr. Lawrence Drew gave £1,500 for one stallion. A large and heavy type is the favourite one, and there has been some intermixture of the Clydesdale with the Shire horse.

Fig. 44.—MR. MANFRED BIDDELL'S SUFFOLK SIRE, "CAPTAIN SNAP."

The Suffolk Punch.

The county of Suffolk boasts a distinct breed of excellent draught horses, which are supposed to have been originally imported from Normandy, and to date back to an earlier time, when that country was invaded and settled by the Norsemen of Scandinavia. The chief feature of the Suffolk Punch, which at once distinguishes it as a breed, is the colour, which is chestnut or light sorrel, with lighter coloured, and almost flaxen, mane and tail. Their form is thick and compact, with short backs and short legs. They are determined pullers, hardy and frugal. The colour of the Suffolk Punch is characteristic of the horse in many parts of the world, but especially in Scandinavia, Northern Europe, and eastwards into the far-off plains of Tartary, where the dun colour is known to prevail.

The Cleveland Bay.

The three breeds last mentioned include the truly distinct draught races of Great Britain. The Cleveland Bay is scarcely a draught horse, although he has been used for ploughing and carting in the district after which he is named. The locality is fixed at the mouth of the Tees, and at the foot of the Cleveland Hills, where a tract of rich land, composed of Lias clay, forms a fertile area north of Thirsk and around Middlesborough.

The Cleveland horse is clean-limbed, and is a bay with black points, and is rather a carriage- than a cart-horse. They are remarkably active, and may be used indiscriminately for ploughing, riding, or trapping. They have, no doubt, originated in the gradual improvement of the horses of the district by successive crossing of high-class blood in which the thorough-bred has had a part. The Cleveland Bay some years ago appeared to be in danger of becoming extinct, and would have done so had it not been for the efforts of the Cleveland Horse Society. The Cleveland mare is suitable for breeding fine carriage-horses of the most approved colour, and may, when put to a thorough-bred, throw a first-rate hunter.

It is described and classified as a coach-horse by Low, who also says : " It has been formed by the same means as the hunter—namely, by the progressive mixture of the blood of the race-horse with original breeds of the country. But a larger class of horse has been used as the basis, and a larger standard adopted by breeders."

The Hackney Horse.

A few years ago the race-horse enjoyed an exclusive use of the term Thorough-bred, which he still retains. All the faster and finer-bred horses were termed " Half-breds," and so much is this still the case that we can only look upon the pure breeding of hunters and roadsters as a new idea.

Richard Lawrence, writing in 1816, says :—" The proper stallion for breeding road horses should be what is called a Half-bred ; " and this continued to be true until recently, and is still true in most cases. Many roadsters, are, however, bred out of stronger mares, and from thorough-bred sires.

In 1883 the Hackney Stud Book Society was formed, to encourage the pure breeding of Norfolk Trotters and Yorkshire Roadsters. The Thorough-bred, or Racer, is not a trotting horse, as is well known. His pace is the gallop, but trotting is an accomplishment of Half-breds and of horses specially bred for the purpose. Among them, the Norfolk Trotters and Yorkshire Roadsters are the most famous, and trotting races have become very fashionable in America.

The object of the Hackney Society is to encourage horses of this type. "A horse bred from Hackneys," says Mr. Anthony Hammond, "whose pedigree can be traced for years, is certain to have action, and action always commands money."

These horses are best when fifteen hands two inches high, and the trot is their strongest pace.

Ponies and Galloways.

A pony should be under twelve hands, or forty-eight inches high, measured carefully by a proper standard at the withers, or shoulder-tops. A Galloway is from twelve to fourteen hands high. The most famous ponies which we possess are those of Shetland or Zetland, Orkney, and the Hebrides; the Welsh ponies; the Exmoor ponies of Devonshire, and the New Forest ponies of Hampshire. The Galloways are named after the small horse of South-Western Scotland.

We are also familiar in this country with the ponies of Norway and Corsica.

These small horses are capable of doing more work than those of larger stature, and are invaluable for a variety of purposes, such as shooting, road work, and saddle work. They are much used for children before they can be trusted to ride a full-sized horse. They are also employed in mines for drawing the loaded trucks to the pit-mouth along the narrow and low passages which extend for miles under ground. These ponies are stabled and live in the mines, and only rarely are allowed a holiday above the surface.

The pony is the result of peculiar conditions of food and climate, and in many cases is known to have been descended from full-sized horses. Thus, in America there are races of ponies, such as the Puno pony, which, like all American horses, is a descendant of animals imported into that continent from Spain in the fifteenth century. Tradition also affirms that at the time of the Armada (1588) many Spanish horses were stranded alive on the shores of the Hebrides and Shetland.

Ponies are always associated with mountains and moors, where a full-sized horse would find it difficult to live. The size becomes reduced, and the severer the climate the smaller is the size. Those of Shetland are often only seven-and-a-half hands high, or even less, and the ordinary height is nine hands. "These little horses in their native islands are left almost in a state of nature until they are caught for use. They have no shelter from the continued storms of tempestuous seas beyond what the crags, ravines, and hill-sides afford; and they scarcely ever receive any food but what they can collect on the sedgy bogs, the heathy hills, and barren shores of the country." (Low.) Such conditions are only favourable for an animal whose size and, therefore, whose requirements in food, are small, and which at the same time is active and hardy; and thus we see that the surroundings or circumstances of the Shetland pony must have constantly tended to reduce his stature and to keep up his hardiness of constitution. The same conditions exist in Norway, the Hebrides, Orkney, North Wales, and in a less degree on Exmoor and the barren heaths of the New Forest. Small islands also appear to be favourable to the development of ponies, of which fact sufficient evidence has been given.

The horse is therefore seen to be capable of great alterations in size, according to the food he is supplied with and the climate to which he is exposed. The small horses of the barren tracts of Arabia, the still smaller ponies of Zetland, and, by contrast, the magnificent horses of the fen-lands of Lincolnshire, which have been bred for hundreds of years on rich pastures and in a temperate climate, are instances which help us to understand the wonderful effect of surroundings, or what naturalists call "environment," on the animal body.

Asses and Mules.

The ass is so well known, and his general character is so similar wherever found in the country, that but little description seems necessary. Asses vary, it is true, in colour, from white to silver grey, and from light to dark brown, also in size to some degree; but in general the English donkey is the same wherever met with. Patient, somewhat stupid, cunning, funny-tempered, but responsive to good treatment, is the donkey. He is the poor man's horse, the companion of the costermonger and small gardener, the children's playmate at home and on the sea-beach—an animal whose appearance often provokes a smile, and whose name has been associated with obstinacy, stupidity, and stolidity in all ages.

The ass is, nevertheless, an object of great interest to

the student. He is valued at a higher rate in many countries than he is here, and attains a larger size and is employed for nobler purposes. Interest in the ass is readily awakened when he is connected with events of sacred and ancient history. He was apparently domesticated before the horse, and if this statement is thought to be doubtful—for both animals have been for ages the willing servants of man—we know that the ancient Jews, and their forefathers, the patriarchs, preferred the ass to the horse. Asses and camels were among the riches of Abraham and Lot, and Balaam's ass is known to all as the only animal which ever opened her mouth, when she, in a miraculous manner, reproved the madness of the prophet. "Saddle me the ass," is a familiar expression in the Old Testament. It was an ass, it will be remembered, upon which our Lord made His triumphal entry into Jerusalem shortly before His crucifixion.

If we are to understand the real character and origin of the ass, we must study him as he appears in far-off regions. He is naturally an inhabitant of desolate places and trackless deserts. There he is free as air, and is of noble nature. His very stubbornness in servitude seems a sort of protest against slavery, for the wild ass is one of the fleetest and freest of beasts. In the beautiful language of Job the ass is selected as one of the most perfect works of the Almighty, and is pictured in the following striking words: "Who hath sent out the wild ass free? or who hath loosed the bonds of the wild ass? whose house he hath made in the wilderness, and the barren land his dwellings. He scorneth the multitude of the city, neither regardeth he the crying of the driver. The range of the mountains is his pasture, and he searcheth after every green thing." This fine description seems at once to indicate the grand freedom of the wild animal, and to hint at the lowliness of the domesticated ass. The "crying of his driver" is a sound as familiar now as in the days of Job, and seems to show that the tame ass, even at that time, required urging. We may also notice in this connection the different language employed when the horse is spoken of as rejoicing in his strength, and saying, "among the trumpets, Ha, ha!"—a form of expression which well imitates the impatient neighing of a charger.

The ass was included by Linnæus in the genus (family) EQUUS, but has been separated into another group by later naturalists, under the name of ASINUS. The horse and the ass are, however, closely allied, as is proved by the fact that they breed together, and produce a sterile offspring, known as the mule.

The wild ass is so well described in the quotation from Job above given that we should only be able to repeat it in other words if we wished to say more. He, in colour and form, resembles the larger varieties of the domesticated animal, and chiefly differs from them in his proverbial wildness. He is known by the Persians as Gor, and this name, coupled with Khur, the Persian name for an ass, forms Gor-Khur, by which the wild ass is known in various countries of the East.

The wild ass abounds in Africa, above the cataracts of the Nile, and is there, as in Asia, an inhabitant of the desert, and is fleet of foot and difficult to capture.

The finest domesticated asses are found in Greece, Italy, and Spain, and also in the old Poitou province of

France. Specimens in the possession of Mr. C. L. Sutherland, at Coombe, Croydon, seen by the author, rivalled the horse in stature. They were about or above fifteen hands high, with splendidly long ears, fine heads, and massive carcases.

It is from these fine asses of Southern Europe that the best mules are bred. The undersized mule which is often

Fig. 45.—A MULE OF THE MIDI.

to be seen in England gives but a poor idea of what this strange animal may become under favourable circumstances. Mr. Sutherland has done a good work in encouraging the breeding of really good mules, and many of them in his possession are as large as horses, and of wonderful power. They are more frugal: that is, can thrive on poorer diet than a horse requires, and they live to a very great age. The best mules are bred from the male ass and mare, as the mother appears to give the external form. Those bred from female asses are longer in the ears, of less beautiful form, and duller in temperament.

The mule is the favourite beast of burden in Spain. They are of various classes, some being suitable for draught purposes, while others of more slender form and finer action are used for the saddle, and are employed by persons of wealth in preference to horses. The mule is wonderfully sure-footed, like the ass. In all mountainous countries, of which Spain is a good example, the mule is invaluable. He can carry his rider safely over mountain passes which appear inaccessible. He can climb slippery ledges of rock overhanging fearful precipices, and when he has arrived at the summit he makes his descent with equal care and safety, often drawing his four feet together, and sliding down steep ravines with fearful rapidity, but instinctive exactness, arriving safely with his burden at the bottom of the perilous path. In transporting merchandise across the dreadful cliffs of the Cordilleras, no animal can be compared with the mule.

In addition to the good qualities already enumerated, the mule is blessed with a constitution wonderfully free from the many diseases to which the horse is subject. The wonder is that in an enterprising country like England the mule is not more largely used; but we believe that his day is coming, and now that he is better known he is likely to become more generally appreciated.

CHAPTER X.

MANAGEMENT OF HORSES.

To treat of the breeding, rearing, training, and management of horses would be to undertake a work far beyond our original purpose, which is to give a fair idea to the young of our many descriptions of live stock. The subject is so large that bulky volumes have been written upon it. Our attention can, therefore, only be given to the management of farm horses, on the same principle upon which we have treated cattle, sheep, and pigs as farm stock.

The management of all animals is naturally divided into breeding, rearing, and after-management—such as fatting in the case of cattle and sheep, or breaking, training, and using in the case of horses.

Breeding Horses.

This important subject includes the breeding of all descriptions of horses, but we shall treat it generally. Whatever breed of horse may be concerned, the selection of parents is an all-important matter. Everyone who has attempted to write upon this subject has laid stress on the importance of only propagating from thoroughly sound and good parents. This is most necessary, and requires to be taught, because, while no one would deny the truth of this principle many persons do not follow it out in practice, but apparently consider that any horse or mare is good enough to breed foals. Some defects, it is true, are not open to objection, among which may be named those caused by accidents, or such as breaking down under heavy work, for example. Some good authorities go even further than this, and advise that no animals should be bred from which are not in full health and vigour, and free from all defects. Lameness, blindness, malformations, etc., may be due to accidents, it is true, but in some cases there has been a weakness or disposition towards these ailments. A thoroughly strong horse might have resisted the causes of these apparent accidents, and therefore all imperfections should be inquired into. Defects which a horse has inherited, and which showed themselves at the time of his birth, or which have developed with his growth, are called **congenital** defects—*i.e.*, they belong to his constitution, and are therefore liable to re-appear in his offspring. The great principle that *like begets like* runs through all Nature, and hence sound, well-formed, good-tempered, and good-actioned horses are only to be relied upon to produce young of the same good character. The same remark applies to mares as well as stallions.

The mare goes for eleven months with young, and generally foals in May.

Mares employed for breeding may be reasonably worked to within a short time of foaling, and, in the case of farm horses, working on the land in the plough or harrow is considered more suitable than travelling in shafts or on the road. For the last month it is advisable to turn her out during the day, and bring her into a large loose box at night. Mares usually foal without assistance, and are rarely seen to produce their young.

After foaling, mares should not be worked for a month; but as the weather is usually fairly warm, she may be turned out into the pastures night and day, unless, indeed, the nights are cold, when she and her foal ought to be housed. The foal ought always to have free access to the mare. This, of course, must be the case as long as the two are turned out together; but when mares are taken up for work they are often over-heated through their exertions, and the milk becomes disordered and sour; the consequence is that the foal scours, and sometimes dies. A more natural system is to allow the foal to follow its dam even when she is at the plough, and it can then suck at short intervals or whenever it feels so disposed. Foals soon learn to eat grass, and are weaned at Michaelmas.

Treatment of Weanling Colts.

The best situation for young colts or fillies after weaning is rough pastures, where there is an abundance of grass upon which they can live during their first winter. Such a pasture, with a hovel into which the young animals can retire and receive a little corn and hay, is really all that is necessary. As colts are sociable, it is not a good plan to place one by itself; it does better with one or more companions. Colts should be liberally fed with a peck of good oats a week and some sweet hay, especially as the season advances. A few carrots or a swede turnip are also wholesome additions to the grass which forms the staple of their food.

Treatment of Yearling Colts.

When a foal has arrived at one year old it is called a yearling, and it is a yearling until it has accomplished its second year, when it becomes a two-year-old, and so on.

During the summer which succeeds its first birthday it runs on grass-land, such as sound dry pasture or marsh. As winter approaches it ought to receive two pecks of oats per week, with hay, as recommended during its first winter.

Treatment of Two-Year-Old Colts.

At two years old cart colts are often broken to light work, such as harrowing in spring corn, more to accustom them to harness and make them handy than to get any profitable work out of them. After a few half-days of such light labour, they should be again turned out for the summer. It is often the custom to break colts gradually to ordinary work in the same autumn, and if they are judiciously employed, and only worked half-days at a time, with frequent holidays, there is no serious objection to the practice. As, however, work often presses, it unfortunately happens that colts are often over-taxed, and damaged for life. A wiser rule is, therefore, to put off breaking-in until the colt has had another winter's run, and to bring him into light work after he is three years old.

Breaking-in Cart Colts.

Foals should be early taught to be led about with a halter, and to lift up their feet when asked by gently lifting a foot and holding it off the ground. They should, in a word, be made docile, and what is called "handy." At two years old they may be bitted or mouthed by allowing them to champ a breaking-bridle for two or three hours a day, and thus to gradually make a tender mouth. Cart colts are seldom lunged around a ring, as is generally done with higher class colts.

At two and a half or three years old a colt may be backed and gently ridden about. One man on either side is a safe precaution when a strong colt is first mounted, and he is then gently led until he becomes accustomed to be ridden. Cart colts are usually introduced to their work by yoking them at once by the side of a steady horse, or between two, and taking the precaution to have plenty of help in case of accident. The horse is easily trained to his work, but great care is requisite that no hitch or accident should happen, such as running away, kicking, entanglement in harness or doorways, as such mishaps are never forgotten. Similarly, the rattle of a cart or vehicle behind a young horse terrifies him a good deal at first, and therefore harnessing to such vehicles should be done carefully and with assistance. Young horses should be taken charge of by experienced men, who never forget the importance of gentle usage, and steady, firm treatment. The breaking-bridle should be kept in the mouth frequently and for long periods, so as to make the mouth thoroughly tender.

Management of Working Horses.

Stabling.—So many kinds of stabling for cart-horses are in use that we may well come to the conclusion that any kind which may be relied upon to keep the animals comfortable will suffice. We have known cart-horses kept in small yards provided with ordinary shedding; in boxes, ten feet by ten feet; in simple sheds, where the animals are tied up side by side, without partitions; and lastly, in ordinary stall stables, in which the horses are divided from each other by proper "travises," or partitions.

All stables should be well lighted, well ventilated, and well drained. They should open and be lighted towards the east. A good stable should be at least seventeen feet wide, and divided as follows from wall to wall:—

	ft.	in.
A trough or manger	1	9
Standing	7	9
Gutter	1	0
Passage behind horses	6	6
	17	0

Each horse is allowed a stall five feet six inches wide, so that for the accommodation of ten horses fifty-five feet in length is required. The stalls should have a slope or fall of three inches from head to gutter, and every stall should be provided with a drain protected by a grating, and should be well paved.

Stables are not provided now with a loft, as it is not thought desirable to store hay above the horses' heads, and that the stable is better open to the roof, as being cooler and more airy. A hay-house may be placed in the centre of a stable devoted to ten or twelve horses, and be provided with locked corn-bins and proper accommodation for chaff as well as long hay. Ventilation is best effected by valved openings placed above the horses' heads and louvered openings in the ridge of the roof. In some cases the ventilators in the front wall are placed low, but this is a matter on which stable managers differ, as it exposes horses to a direct draught. When placed just above the horses' heads the openings may be so contrived as to send the current of cold air upwards. The "travises" should be sufficiently high at the heads to prevent the horses from looking over and fighting or teasing one another. We had a case in which one horse bit a large piece out of his neighbour's tongue for want of this precaution.

In accordance with the plan of having no loft, the mangers are placed low, and the space in front of the horse is divided between rack and manger. In some stables water is laid on so as to be always before the horse, and this point is considered important by many managers. Every stable should be provided with at least one roomy loose box, used for various purposes—such as mares near foaling, or in cases of illness, or when a horse requires prolonged rest. A system of loose boxes is also preferred by many horse-keepers, but it entails a good deal of extra expense in the first instance. A loose box ought not to be less than 14 ft. long and 10 ft. wide, to avoid casting.

Feeding of Farm Horses.

An average-sized horse, in full work, will require, to keep him in health, about 12 lbs. of oats and 8 lbs. of hay daily, together with a little chaff, and access to oat or barley straw, so that he should at all times feel satisfied. The amount of food which a horse requires varies principally with the amount of work he is called upon to perform, and thus various dietaries are recommended, according to the stress of work or the variations of the seasons.

On farms, the four seasons of the year—spring, summer, autumn, and winter—each bring changes in feeding, as different natural foods succeed each other and as the amount of work varies. If we commence the agricultural year after harvest, we shall find a period of activity on most farms. In nearly all cases the preparation for and sowing of winter wheat, and the clearing of stubble, furnish abundance of work for horses. And in others, besides these ordinary employments, there are mangel-wurzels to cart home, winter rye, winter barley, winter vetches to plant, and sometimes winter beans; potatoes to harvest, dung to cart out, and a variety of other work, which together make a busy season. At this period horses ought to be well fed, and it is a matter of observation that if they fall into low condition in the autumn they remain so until the next summer. The food, therefore, must be nutritious and abundant, and may consist of any of the following combinations, each of which represents an allowance for one week:—

$1\frac{1}{2}$ bushels of oats,
$\frac{1}{2}$ bushel of maize,
56 lbs. of hay;

or,

2 bushels of oats,
$\frac{1}{4}$ bushel of beans,
56 lbs. of hay;

or,

1 bushel of maize,
$1\frac{1}{2}$ bushels of oats,
Barley straw (*ad lib.*)

In East Lothian, where Clydesdale horses are kept, it is the custom to give as much as 3½ bushels of home-grown and undressed oats, and hay *ad libitum;* but the hours on a Lothian farm are longer than in Southern England, as horses are out of their stable from six to six, and not, as in Hampshire, from seven to four. Ploughing is also invariably done with two horses, and is usually carried to a depth of from eight to ten inches.

Winter Feeding.—Winter always brings some relief to horses. The days are short, and it is not possible to plough before eight o'clock in the morning or after four in the afternoon. Frosts, snow-storms, and heavy falls of rain, together with gloomy mornings and dark afternoons, and Christmas holidays, all combine to make work lighter and less regular, so that a certain proportion of the corn may be discontinued. The period comprised between December 1st and February 1st, or even March 1st, is unfavourable, as a rule, for tillage operations, and the food of the horses may well be diminished. At this period

> 1 bushel of oats,
> 56 lbs. of hay,

would be a sufficient allowance for a horse for a week; or, if it is thought advisable to save hay,

> 1½ bushels of oats,
> With barley straw,

will answer the same purpose; or,

> 1 bushel of maize,
> With barley straw,

would form a good equivalent.

Spring Feeding of Farm Horses.—With the return of spring comes a revival of occupation for the horses. Odd jobs, such as stone and dirt carting, or hay, straw, or turnip carting for live stock, give place to the more important and serious tasks of getting in the spring corn, or ploughing land for potatoes, mangel, and other early root crops. The allowance of corn must again be increased to the autumn level, and once more a liberal allowance of oats, maize, beans, and hay becomes necessary. (*See* Autumn Feeding of Farm Horses.)

Summer Feeding of Farm Horses.—The busy period of spring is continued through May and June, and in fact until the main bulk of the turnip crop has been sown. After this a lull again occurs in the work of farm horses. Hay-time and harvest are, it is true, periods of arduous work for the men, but the horses are, on the whole, easier worked at these times than when ploughing. Men pitching hay on to and off waggons work harder and more continuously than the horse, which only drags the load. Horses also always have a good deal of food when engaged in harvest work, as they are usually to be seen eating hay or barley ears, or getting frequent little morsels, at such times. Besides, during the summer horses are often turned out on to grass, and the succulent herbage takes away their desire for corn. Many farmers give no hay in the height of summer, and others never exceed one bushel of oats, together with cut clover or vetches and grazing at night. The custom of turning horses out to graze at night is not one much to be recommended, as they frequently catch serious colds and meet with accidents. The manure is also wasted to a great extent, and, unless straw for litter is scarce, we, on the whole, prefer that horses should remain in the stable at night throughout the entire year. Nothing can be worse, for example, than, after horses have been drawing a mowing machine or reaper all day, to be turned out at eight o'clock at night on to a pasture.

General Rules for Feeding Horses.—Having indicated suitable quantities of food for farm horses at all periods of the year, we shall now instruct our youthful readers as to the best modes of feeding. Horses should be fed regularly, and with fair frequency. A good carter should be in his stable early in the morning. In some parts of Lincolnshire the feeding commences at three o'clock, and in no district later than about five o'clock. Taking the latter hour as perhaps sufficiently early, the carter enters his stables, and proceeds to mix a feed of corn (3 to 4 lbs.) with wheat chaff or fine "chop" (chopped straw), and to place it in the mangers before each horse. He then goes to his breakfast, and after an hour returns and waters his horses. They are then rubbed down, harnessed, and in most southern counties leave the stable at seven o'clock. At twelve o'clock they stop for half an hour, and eat a feed of corn and chaff from the nose-bags, which ought to be provided. They then plough or resume work until they unyoke in time to return to the stable at four o'clock. They then are watered, fed with another feed of corn, and the racks are replenished with hay or straw. About eight, or sometimes nine, at night, the carter again enters his stables and makes the horses comfortable for the night, taking care that they have a supply of hay.

"Foddering time," in the northern counties, is a well-known institution, and it is then that the horses are well groomed with wisps of straw, their manes and tails are combed out, and they are well bedded up for the night and fed. Most careful farmers visit the stables at this time, and see that their horses are well attended to.

THE END.

Selections from Cassell & Company's Publications.

Illustrated, Fine-Art, and other Volumes.

Abbeys and Churches of England and Wales, The: Descriptive, Historical, Pictorial. Series II. 21s.
Adventure, The World of. Fully Illustrated. In Three Vols. 9s. each.
Africa and its Explorers, The Story of. By Dr. Robert Brown, F.L.S. Illustrated. Complete in 4 Vols., 7s. 6d. each.
Animals, Popular History of. By Henry Scherren, F.Z.S. With 12 Coloured Plates and other Illustrations. 7s. 6d.
Arabian Nights Entertainments, Cassell's Pictorial. 10s. 6d.
Architectural Drawing. By R. Phené Spiers. Illustrated. 10s. 6d.
Art, The Magazine of. Yearly Vol. With 14 Photogravures or Etchings, a Series of Full-page Plates, and about 400 Illustrations. 21s.
Artistic Anatomy. By Prof. M. Duval. *Cheap Edition.* 3s. 6d.
Astronomy, The Dawn of. A Study of the Temple Worship and Mythology of the Ancient Egyptians. By Prof. J. Norman Lockyer, C.B., F.R.S., &c. Illustrated. 21s.
Atlas, The Universal. A New and Complete General Atlas of the World, with 117 Pages of Maps, in Colours, and a Complete Index to about 125,000 Names. List of Maps, Prices and all Particulars on Application.
Bashkirtseff, Marie, The Journal of. *Cheap Edition.* 7s. 6d.
Bashkirtseff, Marie, The Letters of. 7s. 6d.
Battles of the Nineteenth Century. An Entirely New and Original Work. Illustrated. Vol. I., 9s.
Beetles, Butterflies, Moths, and Other Insects. By A. W. Kappel, F.E.S., and W. Egmont Kirby. With 12 Coloured Plates. 3s. 6d.
"Belle Sauvage" Library, The. Cloth, 2s. each. A list of the Volumes post free on application.
Biographical Dictionary, Cassell's New. *Cheap Edition*, 3s. 6d.
Birds' Nests, Eggs, and Egg-Collecting. By R. Kearton. Illustrated with 16 Coloured Plates. 5s.
Birds' Nests, British: How, Where, and When to Find and Identify Them. By R. Kearton. With an Introduction by Dr. Bowdler Sharpe and upwards of 130 Illustrations of Nests, Eggs, Young, etc., from Photographs by C. Kearton. 21s.
Breech-Loader, The, and How to Use It. By W. W. Greener. Illustrated. New and enlarged edition. 2s. 6d.
Britain's Roll of Glory; or, the Victoria Cross, its Heroes, and their Valour. By D. H. Parry. Illustrated. 7s. 6d.
British Ballads. With Several Hundred Original Illustrations. Complete in Two Vols., cloth, 15s. Half morocco, *price on application.*
British Battles on Land and Sea. By James Grant. With about 600 Illustrations. Four Vols., 4to, £1 16s.; *Library Edition,* £2.
Butterflies and Moths, European. With 61 Coloured Plates. 35s.
Canaries and Cage-Birds, The Illustrated Book of. With 56 Facsimile Coloured Plates, 35s. Half-morocco, £2 5s.
Captain Horn, The Adventures of. By Frank Stockton. 6s.
Capture of the "Estrella," The. A Tale of the Slave Trade. By Commander Claude Harding, R.N. 5s.
Cassell's Family Magazine. Yearly Vol. Illustrated. 7s. 6d.
Cathedrals, Abbeys, and Churches of England and Wales. Descriptive, Historical, Pictorial. *Popular Edition.* Two Vols. 25s.
Cats and Kittens. By Henriette Ronner. With Portrait and 13 Full-page Photogravure Plates and numerous Illustrations. £2 2s.
Chums. The Illustrated Paper for Boys. Yearly Volume, 8s.
Cities of the World. Four Vols. Illustrated. 7s. 6d. each.
Civil Service, Guide to Employment in the. Entirely New Edition. Paper, 1s. Cloth, 1s. 6d.
Clinical Manuals for Practitioners and Students of Medicine. A List of Volumes forwarded post free on application to the Publishers.

Selections from Cassell & Company's Publications.

Colour. By Prof. A. H. CHURCH. With Coloured Plates. 3s. 6d.
Commons and Forests, English. By the Rt. Hon. G. SHAW-LEFEVRE, M.P. With Maps. 10s. 6d.
Cook, The Thorough Good. By GEORGE AUGUSTUS SALA. 21s.
Cookery, A Year's. By PHYLLIS BROWNE. 3s. 6d.
Cookery Book, Cassell's New Universal. By LIZZIE HERITAGE. With 12 Coloured Plates and other Illustrations. Strongly bound in Half-leather. 1,344 pages. 6s.
Cookery, Cassell's Shilling. 110*th Thousand*. 1s.
Cookery, Vegetarian. By A. G. PAYNE. 1s. 6d.
Cooking by Gas, The Art of. By MARIE J. SUGG. Illustrated. 2s.
Cottage Gardening, Poultry, Bees, Allotments, Etc. Edited by W. ROBINSON. Illustrated. Half-yearly Volumes, 2s. 6d. each.
Count Cavour and Madame de Circourt. Some Unpublished Correspondence. Translated by A. J. BUTLER. Cloth gilt, 10s. 6d.
Countries of the World, The. By ROBERT BROWN, M.A., Ph.D., &c. *Cheap Edition.* Profusely Illustrated. Vol. I., 6s.
Cyclopædia, Cassell's Concise. Brought down to the latest date. With about 600 Illustrations. *Cheap Edition.* 7s. 6d.
Cyclopædia, Cassell's Miniature. Containing 30,000 subjects. Cloth, 2s. 6d.; half-roxburgh, 4s.
David Balfour, The Adventures of. By R. L. STEVENSON. Illustrated. Two Vols. 6s. each.
    Part 1.—Kidnapped.   Part 2.—Catriona.
Defoe, Daniel, The Life of. By THOMAS WRIGHT. Illustrated. 21s.
Diet and Cookery for Common Ailments. By a Fellow of the Royal College of Physicians, and PHYLLIS BROWNE. 5s.
Dog, Illustrated Book of the. By VERO SHAW, B.A. With 28 Coloured Plates. Cloth bevelled, 35s.; half-morocco, 45s.
Domestic Dictionary, The. Illustrated. Cloth, 7s. 6d.
Doré Bible, The. With 200 Full-page Illustrations by DORÉ. 15s.
Doré Don Quixote, The. With about 400 Illustrations by GUSTAVE DORÉ. *Cheap Edition.* Bevelled boards, gilt edges, 10s. 6d.
Doré Gallery, The. With 250 Illustrations by DORÉ. 4to, 42s.
Doré's Dante's Inferno. Illustrated by GUSTAVE DORÉ. With Preface by A. J. BUTLER. Cloth gilt or buckram, 7s. 6d.
Doré's Dante's Purgatory and Paradise. Illustrated by GUSTAVE DORÉ. *Cheap Edition.* 7s. 6d.
Doré's Milton's Paradise Lost. Illustrated by DORÉ. 4to, 21s. *Popular Edition.* Cloth gilt or buckram gilt, 7s. 6d.
Dorset, Old. Chapters in the History of the County. By H. J. MOULE, M.A. 10s. 6d.
Dressmaking, Modern, The Elements of. By J. E. DAVIS. Illd. 2s.
Earth, Our, and its Story. By Dr. ROBERT BROWN, F.L.S. With Coloured Plates and numerous Wood Engravings. Three Vols. 9s. each.
Edinburgh, Old and New. With 600 Illustrations. Three Vols. 9s. each.
Egypt: Descriptive, Historical, and Picturesque. By Prof. G. EBERS. With 800 Original Engravings. *Popular Edition.* In Two Vols. 42s.
Electric Current, The. How Produced and How Used. By R. MULLINEUX WALMSLEY, D.Sc., etc. Illustrated. 10s. 6d.
Electricity in the Service of Man. Illustrated. *New and Revised Edition.* 10s. 6d.
Electricity, Practical. By Prof. W. E. AYRTON. 7s. 6d.
Encyclopædic Dictionary, The. In Fourteen Divisional Vols., 10s. 6d. each; or Seven Vols., half-morocco, 21s. each; half-russia, 25s.
England, Cassell's Illustrated History of. With upwards of 2,000 Illustrations. *Revised Edition.* Complete in Eight Vols., 9s. each; cloth gilt, and embossed gilt top and headbanded, £4 net the set.

Selections from Cassell & Company's Publications.

English Dictionary, Cassell's. Giving definitions of more than 100,000 Words and Phrases. *Superior Edition*, 5s. *Cheap Edition*, 3s. 6d.
English Literature, Library of. By Prof. HENRY MORLEY. Complete in Five Vols., 7s. 6d. each.
English Literature, The Dictionary of. By W. DAVENPORT ADAMS. *Cheap Edition*, 7s. 6d.
English Literature, Morley's First Sketch of. *Revised Edition.* 7s. 6d.
English Literature, The Story of. By ANNA BUCKLAND. 3s. 6d.
English Writers. By Prof. HENRY MORLEY. Vols. I. to XI. 5s. each.
Etiquette of Good Society. *New Edition.* Edited and Revised by LADY COLIN CAMPBELL. 1s.; cloth, 1s. 6d.
Fairway Island. By HORACE HUTCHINSON. *Cheap Edition.* 3s. 6d.
Fairy Tales Far and Near. Re-told by Q. Illustrated. 3s. 6d.
Fiction, Cassell's Popular Library of. 3s. 6d. each.

THE AVENGER OF BLOOD. By J. MACLAREN COBBAN.
A MODERN DICK WHITTINGTON. By JAMES PAYN.
THE MAN IN BLACK. By STANLEY WEYMAN.
A BLOT OF INK. Translated by Q. and PAUL M. FRANCKE.
THE MEDICINE LADY. By L. T. MEADE.
OUT OF THE JAWS OF DEATH. By FRANK BARRETT.
THE SNARE OF THE FOWLER. By Mrs. ALEXANDER.
"LA BELLA" AND OTHERS. By EGERTON CASTLE.
LEONA. By Mrs. MOLESWORTH.
FOURTEEN TO ONE, ETC. By ELIZABETH STUART PHELPS.
FATHER STAFFORD. By ANTHONY HOPE.
DR. DUMÁNY'S WIFE. By MAURUS JÓKAI.
THE DOINGS OF RAFFLES HAW. By CONAN DOYLE.

Field Naturalist's Handbook, The. By the Revs. J. G. WOOD and THEODORE WOOD. *Cheap Edition.* 2s. 6d.
Figuier's Popular Scientific Works. With Several Hundred Illustrations in each. Newly Revised and Corrected. 3s. 6d. each.
THE HUMAN RACE. MAMMALIA. OCEAN WORLD.
THE INSECT WORLD. REPTILES AND BIRDS.
WORLD BEFORE THE DELUGE. THE VEGETABLE WORLD.
Flora's Feast. A Masque of Flowers. Penned and Pictured by WALTER CRANE. With 40 Pages in Colours. 5s.
Football, The Rugby Union Game. Edited by REV. F. MARSHALL. Illustrated. *New and Enlarged Edition.* 7s. 6d.
For Glory and Renown. By D. H. PARRY. Illustrated. 5s.
France, From the Memoirs of a Minister of. By STANLEY WEYMAN. 6s.
Franco-German War, Cassell's History of the. Complete in Two Vols. Containing about 500 Illustrations. 9s. each.
Free Lance in a Far Land, A. By HERBERT COMPTON. 6s.
Garden Flowers, Familiar. By SHIRLEY HIBBERD. With Coloured Plates by F. E. HULME, F.L.S. Complete in Five Series. 12s. 6d. each.
Gardening, Cassell's Popular. Illustrated. Four Vols. 5s. each.
Gazetteer of Great Britain and Ireland, Cassell's. Illustrated. Vols. I. and II. 7s. 6d. each.
Gladstone, William Ewart, The People's Life of. Illustrated. 1s.
Gleanings from Popular Authors. Two Vols. With Original Illustrations 4to, 9s. each. Two Vols. in One, 15s.
Gulliver's Travels. With 88 Engravings by MORTEN. *Cheap Edition.* Cloth, 3s. 6d.; cloth gilt, 5s.
Gun and its Development, The. By W. W. GREENER. With 500 Illustrations. 10s. 6d.
Heavens, The Story of the. By Sir ROBERT STAWELL BALL, LL.D., F.R.S., F.R.A.S. With Coloured Plates. *Popular Edition.* 12s. 6d.
Heroes of Britain in Peace and War. With 300 Original Illustrations. Two Vols., 3s. 6d. each; or One Vol., 7s. 6d.
Highway of Sorrow, The. By HESBA STRETTON and ******** 6s

Selections from Cassell & Company's Publications.

Hispaniola Plate (1683-1893). By JOHN BLOUNDELLE-BURTON. 6s.
Historic Houses of the United Kingdom. Profusely Illustrated. 10s. 6d.
History, A Foot-note to. Eight Years of Trouble in Samoa. By ROBERT LOUIS STEVENSON. 6s.
Home Life of the Ancient Greeks, The. Translated by ALICE ZIMMERN. Illustrated. *Cheap Edition.* 5s.
Horse, The Book of the. By SAMUEL SIDNEY. With 17 Full-page Collotype Plates of Celebrated Horses of the Day, and numerous other Illustrations. Cloth, 15s.
Horses and Dogs. By O. EERELMAN. With Descriptive Text. Translated from the Dutch by CLARA BELL. With Photogravure Frontispiece, 12 Exquisite Collotypes, and several full page and other engravings in the text. 25s. net.
Houghton, Lord: The Life, Letters, and Friendships of Richard Monckton Milnes, First Lord Houghton. By Sir WEMYSS REID. In Two Vols., with Two Portraits. 32s.
Household, Cassell's Book of the. Complete in Four Vols. 5s. each. Four Vols. in Two, half-morocco, 25s.
Hygiene and Public Health. By B. ARTHUR WHITELEGGE, M.D. 7s. 6d.
Impregnable City, The. By MAX PEMBERTON. 6s.
India, Cassell's History of. By JAMES GRANT. With about 400 Illustrations. Two Vols., 9s. each. One Vol., 15s.
Iron Pirate, The. By MAX PEMBERTON. Illustrated. 5s.
Island Nights' Entertainments. By R. L. STEVENSON. Illustrated. 6s.
Kennel Guide, The Practical. By Dr. GORDON STABLES. 1s.
Khiva, A Ride to. By Col. FRED BURNABY. *New Edition.* With Portrait and Seven Illustrations. 3s. 6d.
King George, In the Days of. By COL. PERCY GROVES. Illd. 1s. 6d.
King's Hussar, A. Edited by HERBERT COMPTON. 6s.
Ladies' Physician, The. By a London Physician. *Cheap Edition, Revised and Enlarged.* 3s. 6d.
Lady Biddy Fane, The Admirable. By FRANK BARRETT. *New Edition.* With 12 Full-page Illustrations. 6s.
Lady's Dressing-room, The. Translated from the French of BARONESS STAFFE by LADY COLIN CAMPBELL. 3s. 6d.
Letters, the Highway of, and its Echoes of Famous Footsteps. By THOMAS ARCHER. Illustrated. 10s. 6d.
Letts's Diaries and other Time-saving Publications published exclusively by CASSELL & COMPANY. (*A list free on application.*)
'Lisbeth. A Novel. By LESLIE KEITH. 6s.
List, ye Landsmen! By W. CLARK RUSSELL. 6s.
Little Minister, The. By J. M. BARRIE. *Illustrated Edition.* 6s.
Little Squire, The. By Mrs. HENRY DE LA PASTURE. 3s. 6d.
Llollandllaff Legends, The. By LOUIS LLOLLANDLLAFF. 1s.; cloth. 2s.
Lobengula, Three Years With, and Experiences in South Africa. By J. COOPER-CHADWICK. *Cheap Edition,* 2s. 6d.
Locomotive Engine, The Biography of a. By HENRY FRITH. 3s. 6d.
Loftus, Lord Augustus, The Diplomatic Reminiscences of. First and Second Series. Two Vols., each with Portrait, 32s. each Series.
London, Greater. By EDWARD WALFORD. Two Vols. With about 400 Illustrations. 9s. each.
London, Old and New. Six Vols., each containing about 200 Illustrations and Maps. Cloth, 9s. each.
Lost on Du Corrig; or, 'Twixt Earth and Ocean. By STANDISH O'GRADY. With 8 Full-page Illustrations. 5s.
Medicine, Manuals for Students of. (*A List forwarded post free.*)
Modern Europe, A History of. By C. A. FYFFE, M.A. *Cheap Edition in One Volume,* 10s. 6d. Library Edition. Illustrated. 3 Vols., 7s. 6d. each.
Mount Desolation. An Australian Romance. By W. CARLTON DAWE. *Cheap Edition.* 3s. 6d.

Selections from Cassell & Company's Publications.

Music, Illustrated History of. By EMIL NAUMANN. Edited by the Rev. Sir F. A. GORE OUSELEY, Bart. Illustrated. Two Vols. 31s. 6d.
National Library, Cassell's. In 214 Volumes. Paper covers, 3d.; cloth, 6d. (*A Complete List of the Volumes post free on application.*)
Natural History, Cassell's Concise. By E. PERCEVAL WRIGHT, M.A., M.D., F.L.S. With several Hundred Illustrations. 7s. 6d.
Natural History, Cassell's New. Edited by Prof. P. MARTIN DUNCAN, M.B., F.R.S., F.G.S. Complete in Six Vols. With about 2,000 Illustrations. Cloth, 9s. each.
Nature's Wonder Workers. By KATE R. LOVELL. Illustrated. 3s. 6d.
New England Boyhood, A. By EDWARD E. HALE. 3s. 6d.
New Zealand, Picturesque. With Preface by Sir W. B. PERCEVAL, K.C.M.G. Illustrated. 6s.
Nursing for the Home and for the Hospital, A Handbook of. By CATHERINE J. WOOD. *Cheap Edition.* 1s. 6d.; cloth, 2s.
Nursing of Sick Children, A Handbook for the. By CATHERINE J. WOOD. 2s. 6d.
Ohio, The New. A Story of East and West. By EDWARD E. HALE. 6s.
Oil Painting, A Manual of. By the Hon. JOHN COLLIER. 2s. 6d.
Old Maids and Young. By E. D'ESTERRE KEELING. 6s.
Old Boy's Yarns, An. By HAROLD AVERY. With 8 Plates. 3s. 6d.
Our Own Country. Six Vols. With 1,200 Illustrations. 7s. 6d. each.
Painting, The English School of. *Cheap Edition.* 3s. 6d.
Painting, Practical Guides to. With Coloured Plates:—

MARINE PAINTING. 5s.	WATER-COLOUR PAINTING. 5s.
ANIMAL PAINTING. 5s.	NEUTRAL TINT. 5s.
CHINA PAINTING. 5s.	SEPIA, in Two Vols., 3s. each; or in One Vol., 5s.
FIGURE PAINTING. 7s. 6d.	
ELEMENTARY FLOWER PAINTING. 3s.	FLOWERS, AND HOW TO PAINT THEM. 5s.

Paris, Old and New. A Narrative of its History, its People, and its Places. By H. SUTHERLAND EDWARDS. Profusely Illustrated. Complete in Two Vols., 9s. each; or gilt edges, 10s. 6d. each.
Peoples of the World, The. In Six Vols. By Dr. ROBERT BROWN. Illustrated. 7s. 6d. each.
Photography for Amateurs. By T. C. HEPWORTH. *Enlarged and Revised Edition.* Illustrated. 1s.; or cloth, 1s. 6d.
Phrase and Fable, Dr. Brewer's Dictionary of. Giving the Derivation, Source, or Origin of Common Phrases, Allusions, and Words that have a Tale to Tell. *Entirely New and Greatly Enlarged Edition.* 10s. 6d.
Picturesque America. Complete in Four Vols., with 48 Exquisite Steel Plates and about 800 Original Wood Engravings. £2 2s. each. *Popular Edition*, Vols. I. & II., 18s. each. [the Set.
Picturesque Canada. With 600 Original Illustrations. Two Vols. £6 6s.
Picturesque Europe. Complete in Five Vols. Each containing 13 Exquisite Steel Plates, from Original Drawings, and nearly 200 Original Illustrations. Cloth, £21; half-morocco, £31 10s.; morocco gilt, £52 10s. POPULAR EDITION. In Five Vols., 18s. each.
Picturesque Mediterranean, The. With Magnificent Original Illustrations by the leading Artists of the Day. Complete in Two Vols. £2 2s. each.
Pigeon Keeper, The Practical. By LEWIS WRIGHT. Illustrated. 3s. 6d.
Pigeons, Fulton's Book of. Edited by LEWIS WRIGHT. Revised, Enlarged and supplemented by the Rev. W. F. LUMLEY. With 50 Full page Illustrations. *Popular Edition.* In One Vol., 10s. 6d.
Planet, The Story of Our. By T. G. BONNEY, D.Sc., LL.D., F.R.S., F.S.A., F.G.S. With Coloured Plates and Maps and about 100 Illustrations. 31s. 6d.
Pocket Library, Cassell's. Cloth, 1s. 4d. each.
  A King's Diary. By PERCY WHITE.
  A White Baby. By JAMES WELSH.
  The Little Huguenot. By MAX PEMBERTON.
  A Whirl Asunder. By GERTRUDE ATHERTON.

Selections from Cassell & Company's Publications.

Poems, Aubrey de Vere's. A Selection. Edited by J. DENNIS. 3s. 6d.
Poets, Cassell's Miniature Library of the. Price 1s. each Vol.
Pomona's Travels. By FRANK R. STOCKTON. Illustrated. 5s.
Portrait Gallery, The Cabinet. Complete in Five Series, each containing 36 Cabinet Photographs of Eminent Men and Women. 15s. each.
Portrait Gallery, Cassell's Universal. Containing 240 Portraits of Celebrated Men and Women of the Day. With brief Memoirs and *facsimile* Autographs. Cloth, 6s.
Poultry Keeper, The Practical. By L. WRIGHT. Illustrated. 3s. 6d.
Poultry, The Book of. By LEWIS WRIGHT. *Popular Edition.* 10s. 6d.
Poultry, The Illustrated Book of. By LEWIS WRIGHT. With Fifty Coloured Plates. *New and Revised Edition.* Cloth, gilt edges (*Price on application*). Half-morocco, £2 2s.
Prison Princess, A. By Major ARTHUR GRIFFITHS. 6s.
"Punch," The History of. By M. H. SPIELMANN. With upwards of 160 Illustrations, Portraits, and Facsimiles. Cloth, 16s.; *Large Paper Edition*, £2 2s. net.
Q's Works, Uniform Edition of. 5s. each.

Dead Man's Rock.	The Astonishing History of Troy Town.
The Splendid Spur.	"I Saw Three Ships," and other Winter's Tales.
The Blue Pavilions.	Noughts and Crosses.
	The Delectable Duchy.

Queen Summer; or, The Tourney of the Lily and the Rose. With Forty Pages of Designs in Colours by WALTER CRANE. 6s.
Queen, The People's Life of their. By Rev. E. J. HARDY, M.A. 1s.
Queen Victoria, The Life and Times of. By ROBERT WILSON. Complete in Two Vols. With numerous Illustrations. 9s. each.
Queen's Scarlet, The. By G. MANVILLE FENN. Illustrated. 5s.
Rabbit-Keeper, The Practical. By CUNICULUS. Illustrated. 3s. 6d.
Railways, Our. Their Origin, Development, Incident, and Romance. By JOHN PENDLETON. Illustrated. 2 Vols., 24s.
Railway Guides, Official Illustrated. With Illustrations, Maps, &c. Price 1s. each; or in cloth, 2s. each.

LONDON AND NORTH WESTERN RAILWAY.	GREAT EASTERN RAILWAY.
GREAT WESTERN RAILWAY.	LONDON AND SOUTH WESTERN RAILWAY.
MIDLAND RAILWAY.	LONDON, BRIGHTON AND SOUTH COAST RAILWAY.
GREAT NORTHERN RAILWAY.	SOUTH-EASTERN RAILWAY.

Railway Guides, Official Illustrated. Abridged and Popular Editions. Paper covers, 3d. each.

GREAT EASTERN RAILWAY.	LONDON AND SOUTH WESTERN RAILWAY.
LONDON AND NORTH WESTERN RAILWAY.	

Railway Library, Cassell's. Crown 8vo, boards, 2s. each. (*A List of the Vols. post free on application.*)
Red Terror, The. A Story of the Paris Commune. By EDWARD KING. Illustrated. 3s. 6d.
Rivers of Great Britain: Descriptive, Historical, Pictorial.
  THE ROYAL RIVER: The Thames, from Source to Sea. 16s.
  RIVERS OF THE EAST COAST. *Popular Edition*, 16s.
Robinson Crusoe, Cassell's New Fine-Art Edition of. 7s. 6d.
Romance, The World of. Illustrated. Cloth, 9s.
Royal Academy Pictures, 1895. With upwards of 200 magnificent reproductions of Pictures in the Royal Academy of 1895. 7s. 6d.
Russo-Turkish War, Cassell's History of. With about 500 Illustrations. Two Vols. 9s. each.
Sala, George Augustus, The Life and Adventures of. By Himself. In Two Vols., demy 8vo, cloth, 32s.
Saturday Journal, Cassell's. Yearly Volume, cloth, 7s. 6d.

Selections from Cassell & Company's Publications.

Science Series, The Century. Consisting of Biographies of Eminent Scientific Men of the present Century. Edited by Sir HENRY ROSCOE, D.C.L., F.R.S. Crown 8vo, 3s. 6d. each.
    John Dalton and the Rise of Modern Chemistry. By Sir HENRY E. ROSCOE, F.R.S.
    Major Rennell, F.R.S., and the Rise of English Geography. By CLEMENTS R. MARKHAM, C.B., F.R.S., President of the Royal Geographical Society.
    Justus Von Liebig: His Life and Work. By W. A. SHENSTONE, F.I.C.
    The Herschels and Modern Astronomy. By MISS AGNES M. CLERKE.
    Charles Lyell: His Life and Work. By Professor T. G. BONNEY, F.R.S.
Science for All. Edited by Dr. ROBERT BROWN. Five Vols. 9s. each.
Scotland, Picturesque and Traditional. A Pilgrimage with Staff and Knapsack. By G. E. EYRE-TODD. 6s.
Sea, The Story of the. An Entirely New and Original Work. Edited by Q. Illustrated. Vol. I. 9s.
Sea Wolves, The. By MAX PEMBERTON. Illustrated. 6s.
Shadow of a Song, The. A Novel. By CECIL HARLEY. 5s.
Shaftesbury, The Seventh Earl of, K.G., The Life and Work of. By EDWIN HODDER. *Cheap Edition.* 3s. 6d.
Shakespeare, The Plays of. Edited by Professor HENRY MORLEY. Complete in Thirteen Vols., cloth, 21s.; half-morocco, cloth sides, 42s.
Shakespeare, Cassell's Quarto Edition. Containing about 600 Illustrations by H. C. SELOUS. Complete in Three Vols., cloth gilt, £3 3s.
Shakespeare, The England of. *New Edition.* By E. GOADBY. With Full-page Illustrations. 2s. 6d.
Shakspere's Works. *Édition de Luxe.*
    "King Henry VIII." Illustrated by SIR JAMES LINTON, P.R.I. (*Price on application.*)
    "Othello." Illustrated by FRANK DICKSEE, R.A. £3 10s.
    "King Henry IV." Illustrated by EDUARD GRÜTZNER. £3 10s.
    "As You Like It." Illustrated by ÉMILE BAYARD. £3 10s.
Shakspere, The Leopold. With 400 Illustrations. *Cheap Edition.* 3s. 6d. Cloth gilt, gilt edges, 5s.; Roxburgh, 7s. 6d.
Shakspere, The Royal. With Steel Plates and Wood Engravings. Three Vols. 15s. each.
Sketches, The Art of Making and Using. From the French of G. FRAIPONT. By CLARA BELL. With 50 Illustrations. 2s. 6d.
Smuggling Days and Smuggling Ways. By Commander the Hon. HENRY N. SHORE, R.N. With numerous Illustrations. 7s. 6d.
Social England. A Record of the Progress of the People. By various writers. Edited by H. D. TRAILL, D.C.L. Vols. I., II., & III., 15s. each. Vol. IV., 17s.
Social Welfare, Subjects of. By Rt. Hon. LORD PLAYFAIR, K.C.B. 7s. 6d.
Sports and Pastimes, Cassell's Complete Book of. *Cheap Edition.* With more than 900 Illustrations. Medium 8vo, 992 pages, cloth, 3s. 6d.
Squire, The. By Mrs. PARR. *Popular Edition.* 6s.
Standishs of High Acre, The. A Novel. By GILBERT SHELDON. Two Vols. 21s.
Star-Land. By Sir R. S. BALL, LL.D., &c. Illustrated. 6s.
Statesmen, Past and Future. 6s.
Story of Francis Cludde, The. By STANLEY J. WEYMAN. 6s.
Story Poems. For Young and Old. Edited by E. DAVENPORT. 3s. 6d.
Sun, The. By Sir ROBERT STAWELL BALL, LL.D., F.R.S., F.R.A.S. With Eight Coloured Plates and other Illustrations. 21s.
Sunshine Series, Cassell's. 1s. each.
    (*A List of the Volumes post free on application.*)
Thackeray in America, With. By EYRE CROWE, A.R.A. Ill. 10s. 6d.
The "Treasure Island" Series. *Illustrated Edition.* 3s. 6d. each.

Treasure Island. By ROBERT LOUIS STEVENSON.	The Black Arrow. By ROBERT LOUIS STEVENSON.
The Master of Ballantrae. By ROBERT LOUIS STEVENSON.	King Solomon's Mines. By H. RIDER HAGGARD.

Selections from Cassell & Company's Publications.

Things I have Seen and People I have Known. By G. A. SALA. With Portrait and Autograph. 2 Vols. 21s.

Tidal Thames, The. By GRANT ALLEN. With India Proof Impressions of Twenty magnificent Full-page Photogravure Plates, and with many other Illustrations in the Text after Original Drawings by W. L. WYLLIE, A.R.A. Half morocco. £5 15s. 6d.

Tiny Luttrell. By E. W. HORNUNG. *Popular Edition.* 6s.

To Punish the Czar: a Story of the Crimea. By HORACE HUTCHINSON. Illustrated. 3s. 6d.

Treatment, The Year-Book of, for 1896. A Critical Review for Practitioners of Medicine and Surgery. *Twelfth Year of Issue.* 7s. 6d.

Trees, Familiar. By G. S. BOULGER, F.L.S. Two Series. With 40 full-page Coloured Plates by W. H. J. BOOT. 12s. 6d. each.

Tuxter's Little Maid. By G. B. BURGIN. 6s.

"Unicode": the Universal Telegraphic Phrase Book. *Desk or Pocket Edition.* 2s. 6d.

United States, Cassell's History of the. By EDMUND OLLIER. With 600 Illustrations. Three Vols. 9s. each.

Universal History, Cassell's Illustrated. Four Vols. 9s. each.

Vision of Saints, A. By Sir LEWIS MORRIS. With 20 Full-page Illustrations. Crown 4to, cloth, 10s. 6d. *Non-illustrated Edition*, 6s.

Wandering Heath. Short Stories. By Q. 6s.

War and Peace, Memories and Studies of. By ARCHIBALD FORBES. 16s.

Westminster Abbey, Annals of. By E. T. BRADLEY (Mrs. A. MURRAY SMITH). Illustrated. With a Preface by Dean BRADLEY. 63s.

White Shield, The. By BERTRAM MITFORD. 6s.

Wild Birds, Familiar. By W. SWAYSLAND. Four Series. With 40 Coloured Plates in each. (Sold in sets only; price on application.)

Wild Flowers, Familiar. By F. E. HULME, F.L.S., F.S.A. Five Series. With 40 Coloured Plates in each. (In sets only; price on application.)

Wild Flowers Collecting Book. In Six Parts, 4d. each.

Wild Flowers Drawing and Painting Book. In Six Parts, 4d. each.

Windsor Castle, The Governor's Guide to. By the Most Noble the MARQUIS OF LORNE, K.T. Profusely Illustrated. Limp Cloth, 1s. Cloth boards, gilt edges, 2s.

Wit and Humour, Cassell's New World of. With New Pictures and New Text. 6s.

With Claymore and Bayonet. By Col. PERCY GROVES. Illd. 5s.

Wood, Rev. J. G., Life of. By the Rev. THEODORE WOOD. Extra crown 8vo, cloth. *Cheap Edition.* 3s. 6d.

Work. The Illustrated Weekly Journal for Mechanics. Vol. IX., 4s.

"Work" Handbooks. Practical Manuals prepared *under the direction of* PAUL N. HASLUCK, Editor of *Work*. Illustrated. 1s. each.

World Beneath the Waters, A. By Rev. GERARD BANCKS. 3s. 6d.

World of Wonders. Two Vols. With 400 Illustrations. 7s. 6d. each.

Wrecker, The. By R. L. STEVENSON and L. OSBOURNE. Illustrated. 6s.

Yule Tide. Cassell's Christmas Annual. 1s.

ILLUSTRATED MAGAZINES.

The Quiver. Monthly, 6d.

Cassell's Family Magazine. Monthly, 6d.

"Little Folks" Magazine. Monthly, 6d.

The Magazine of Art. Monthly, 1s. 4d.

"Chums." Illustrated Paper for Boys. Weekly, 1d.; Monthly, 6d.

Cassell's Saturday Journal. Weekly, 1d.; Monthly, 6d.

Work. Weekly, 1d.; Monthly, 6d.

Cottage Gardening. Weekly, ½d.; Monthly, 3d.

CASSELL & COMPANY, LIMITED, *Ludgate Hill, London.*

Selections from Cassell & Company's Publications.

Bibles and Religious Works.

Bible Biographies. Illustrated. 2s. 6d. each.
   The Story of Moses and Joshua. By the Rev. J. TELFORD.
   The Story of the Judges. By the Rev. J. WYCLIFFE GEDGE.
   The Story of Samuel and Saul. By the Rev. D. C. TOVEY.
   The Story of David. By the Rev. J. WILD.
   The Story of Joseph. Its Lessons for To-Day. By the Rev. GEORGE BAINTON.
   The Story of Jesus. In Verse. By J. R. MACDUFF, D.D.

Bible, Cassell's Illustrated Family. With 900 Illustrations. Leather, gilt edges, £2 10s.

Bible Educator, The. Edited by the Very Rev. Dean PLUMPTRE, D.D. With Illustrations, Maps, &c. Four Vols., cloth, 6s. each.

Bible Manual, Cassell's Illustrated. By the Rev. ROBERT HUNTER, LL.D. *Illustrated.* 7s. 6d.

Bible Student in the British Museum, The. By the Rev. J. G. KITCHIN, M.A. *New and Revised Edition.* 1s. 4d.

Biblewomen and Nurses. Yearly Volume. Illustrated. 3s.

Bunyan, Cassell's Illustrated. With 200 Original Illustrations. *Cheap Edition.* 7s. 6d.

Bunyan's Pilgrim's Progress. Illustrated throughout. Cloth, 3s. 6d.; cloth gilt, gilt edges, 5s.

Child's Bible, The. With 200 Illustrations. 150*th Thousand.* 7s. 6d.

Child's Life of Christ, The. With 200 Illustrations. 7s. 6d.

"Come, ye Children." Illustrated. By Rev. BENJAMIN WAUGH. 3s. 6d.

Conquests of the Cross. Illustrated. In 3 Vols. 9s. each.

Doré Bible. With 238 Illustrations by GUSTAVE DORÉ. Small folio, best morocco, gilt edges, £15. *Popular Edition.* With 200 Illustrations. 15s.

Early Days of Christianity, The. By the Very Rev. Dean FARRAR, D.D., F.R.S. LIBRARY EDITION. Two Vols., 24s.; morocco, £2 2s. POPULAR EDITION. Complete in One Volume, cloth, 6s.; cloth, gilt edges, 7s. 6d.; Persian morocco, 10s. 6d.; tree-calf, 15s.

Family Prayer-Book, The. Edited by Rev. Canon GARBETT. M.A., and Rev. S. MARTIN. With Full page Illustrations. *New Edition.* Cloth, 7s. 6d.

Gleanings after Harvest. Studies and Sketches by the Rev. JOHN R. VERNON, M.A. Illustrated. 6s.

"Graven in the Rock." By the Rev. Dr. SAMUEL KINNS, F.R.A.S., Author of "Moses and Geology." Illustrated. 12s. 6d.

"Heart Chords." A Series of Works by Eminent Divines. Bound in cloth, red edges, One Shilling each.

MY BIBLE. By the Right Rev. W. BOYD CARPENTER, Bishop of Ripon.	MY GROWTH IN DIVINE LIFE. By the Rev. Preb. REYNOLDS, M.A.
MY FATHER. By the Right Rev. ASHTON OXENDEN, late Bishop of Montreal.	MY SOUL. By the Rev. P. B. POWER, M.A.
MY WORK FOR GOD. By the Right Rev. Bishop COTTERILL.	MY HEREAFTER. By the Very Rev. Dean BICKERSTETH.
MY OBJECT IN LIFE. By the Very Rev. Dean FARRAR, D.D.	MY WALK WITH GOD. By the Very Rev. Dean MONTGOMERY.
MY ASPIRATIONS. By the Rev. G. MATHESON, D.D.	MY AIDS TO THE DIVINE LIFE. By the Very Rev. Dean BOYLE.
MY EMOTIONAL LIFE. By the Rev. Preb. CHADWICK, D.D.	MY SOURCES OF STRENGTH. By the Rev. E. E. JENKINS, M.A., Secretary of Wesleyan Missionary Society.
MY BODY. By the Rev. Prof. W. G. BLAIKIE, D.D.	

Helps to Belief. A Series of Helpful Manuals on the Religious Difficulties of the Day. Edited by the Rev. TEIGNMOUTH SHORE, M.A., Canon of Worcester. Cloth, 1s. each.

CREATION. By Harvey Goodwin, D.D., late Bishop of Carlisle.	PRAYER. By the Rev. Canon Shore, M.A.
THE DIVINITY OF OUR LORD. By the Lord Bishop of Derry.	THE ATONEMENT. By William Connor Magee, D.D., Late Archbishop of York.
MIRACLES. By the Rev. Brownlow Maitland, M.A.	

Selections from Cassell & Company's Publications.

Holy Land and the Bible, The. By the Rev. C. GEIKIE, D.D., LL.D. (Edin.). Two Vols., 24s. *Illustrated Edition*, One Vol., 21s.

Life of Christ, The. By the Very Rev. Dean FARRAR, D.D., F.R.S LIBRARY EDITION. Two Vols. Cloth, 24s.; morocco, 42s. CHEAP ILLUSTRATED EDITION. Cloth, 7s. 6d.; cloth, full gilt, gilt edges, 10s. 6d. POPULAR EDITION (*Revised and Enlarged*), 8vo, cloth, gilt edges, 7s. 6d.; Persian morocco, gilt edges, 10s. 6d.; tree-calf, 15s.

Moses and Geology; or, The Harmony of the Bible with Science. By the Rev. SAMUEL KINNS, Ph.D., F.R.A.S. Illustrated. *New Edition.* 10s. 6d.

My Last Will and Testament. By HYACINTHE LOYSON (Père Hyacinthe). Translated by FABIAN WARE. 1s.; cloth, 1s. 6d.

New Light on the Bible and the Holy Land. By B. T. A. EVETTS, M.A. Illustrated. 21s.

New Testament Commentary for English Readers, The. Edited by Bishop ELLICOTT. In Three Volumes. 21s. each. Vol. I.—The Four Gospels. Vol. II.—The Acts, Romans, Corinthians, Galatians. Vol. III.—The remaining Books of the New Testament.

New Testament Commentary. Edited by Bishop ELLICOTT. Handy Volume Edition. St. Matthew, 3s. 6d. St. Mark, 3s. St. Luke, 3s. 6d. St. John, 3s. 6d. The Acts of the Apostles, 3s. 6d. Romans, 2s. 6d. Corinthians I. and II., 3s. Galatians, Ephesians, and Philippians, 3s. Colossians, Thessalonians, and Timothy, 3s. Titus, Philemon, Hebrews, and James, 3s. Peter, Jude, and John, 3s. The Revelation, 3s. An Introduction to the New Testament, 3s. 6d.

Old Testament Commentary for English Readers, The. Edited by Bishop ELLICOTT. Complete in Five Vols. 21s. each. Vol. I.—Genesis to Numbers. Vol. II. — Deuteronomy to Samuel II. Vol. III.—Kings I. to Esther. Vol. IV.—Job to Isaiah. Vol. V.—Jeremiah to Malachi.

Old Testament Commentary. Edited by Bishop ELLICOTT. Handy Volume Edition. Genesis, 3s. 6d. Exodus, 3s. Leviticus, 3s. Numbers, 2s. 6d. Deuteronomy, 2s. 6d.

Plain Introductions to the Books of the Old Testament. Edited by Bishop ELLICOTT. 3s. 6d.

Plain Introductions to the Books of the New Testament. Edited by Bishop ELLICOTT. 3s. 6d.

Protestantism, The History of. By the Rev. J. A. WYLIE, LL.D. Containing upwards of 600 Original Illustrations. Three Vols. 9s. each.

Quiver Yearly Volume, The. With about 600 Original Illustrations. 7s. 6d.

Religion, The Dictionary of. By the Rev. W. BENHAM, B.D. *Cheap Edition.* 10s. 6d.

St. George for England; and other Sermons preached to Children. By the Rev. T. TEIGNMOUTH SHORE, M.A., Canon of Worcester. 5s.

St. Paul, The Life and Work of. By the Very Rev. Dean FARRAR, D.D., F.R.S. LIBRARY EDITION. Two Vols., cloth, 24s.; calf, 42s. ILLUSTRATED EDITION, complete in One Volume, with about 300 Illustrations, £1 1s.; morocco, £2 2s. POPULAR EDITION. One Volume, 8vo, cloth, 6s.; cloth, gilt edges, 7s. 6d.; Persian morocco, 10s. 6d.; tree-calf, 15s.

Shall We Know One Another in Heaven? By the Rt. Rev. J. C. RYLE, D.D., Bishop of Liverpool. *Cheap Edition.* Paper covers, 6d.

Searchings in the Silence. By Rev. GEORGE MATHESON, D.D. 3s. 6d.

"Sunday," Its Origin, History, and Present Obligation. By the Ven. Archdeacon HESSEY, D.C.L. *Fifth Edition.* 7s. 6d.

Twilight of Life, The. Words of Counsel and Comfort for the Aged. By the Rev. JOHN ELLERTON, M.A. 1s. 6d.

Selections from Cassell & Company's Publications.

Educational Works and Students' Manuals.

Agricultural Text-Books, Cassell's. (The "Downton" Series.) Edited by JOHN WRIGHTSON, Professor of Agriculture. Fully Illustrated, 2s. 6d. each.—Farm Crops. By Prof. WRIGHTSON.—Soils and Manures. By J. M. H. MUNRO, D.Sc. (London), F.I.C., F.C.S.—Live Stock. By Prof. WRIGHTSON.
Alphabet, Cassell's Pictorial. 3s. 6d.
Arithmetics, Cassell's "Belle Sauvage." By GEORGE RICKS, B.Sc. Lond. With Test Cards. (*List on application.*)
Atlas, Cassell's Popular. Containing 24 Coloured Maps. 2s. 6d.
Book-Keeping. By THEODORE JONES. For Schools, 2s.; cloth, 3s. For the Million, 2s.; cloth, 3s. Books for Jones's System, 2s.
British Empire Map of the World. By G. R. PARKIN and J. G. BARTHOLOMEW, F.R.G.S. 25s.
Chemistry, The Public School. By J. H. ANDERSON, M.A. 2s. 6d.
Cookery for Schools. By LIZZIE HERITAGE. 6d.
Dulce Domum. Rhymes and Songs for Children. Edited by JOHN FARMER, Editor of "Gaudeamus," &c. Old Notation and Words, 5s. N.B.—The words of the Songs in "Dulce Domum" (with the Airs both in Tonic Sol-fa and Old Notation) can be had in Two Parts, 6d. each.
Euclid, Cassell's. Edited by Prof. WALLACE, M.A. 1s.
Euclid, The First Four Books of. *New Edition.* In paper, 6d.; cloth, 9d.
Experimental Geometry. By PAUL BERT. Illustrated. 1s. 6d.
French, Cassell's Lessons in. *New and Revised Edition.* Parts I. and II., each 2s. 6d.; complete, 4s. 6d. Key, 1s. 6d.
French-English and English-French Dictionary. *Entirely New and Enlarged Edition.* Cloth, 3s. 6d.; superior binding, 5s.
French Reader, Cassell's Public School. By G. S. CONRAD. 2s. 6d.
Gaudeamus. Songs for Colleges and Schools. Edited by JOHN FARMER. 5s. Words only, paper covers, 6d.; cloth, 9d.
German Dictionary, Cassell's New (German-English, English-German). *Cheap Edition.* Cloth, 3s. 6d. *Superior Binding*, 5s.
Hand and Eye Training. By G. RICKS, B.Sc. 2 Vols., with 16 Coloured Plates in each Vol. Cr. 4to, 6s. each. Cards for Class Use, 5 sets, 1s. each.
Hand and Eye Training. By GEORGE RICKS, B.Sc., and JOSEPH VAUGHAN. Illustrated. Vol. I. Designing with Coloured Papers. Vol. II. Cardboard Work. 2s. each. Vol. III. Colour Work and Design, 3s.
Historical Cartoons, Cassell's Coloured. Size 45 in. × 35 in., 2s. each. Mounted on canvas and varnished, with rollers, 5s. each.
Italian Lessons, with Exercises, Cassell's. Cloth, 3s. 6d.
Latin Dictionary, Cassell's New. (Latin-English and English-Latin.) Revised by J. R. V. MARCHANT, M.A., and J. F. CHARLES, B.A. Cloth, 3s. 6d. *Superior Binding*, 5s.
Latin Primer, The First. By Prof. POSTGATE. 1s.
Latin Primer, The New. By Prof. J. P. POSTGATE. 2s. 6d.
Latin Prose for Lower Forms. By M. A. BAYFIELD, M.A. 2s. 6d.
Laws of Every-Day Life. By H. O. ARNOLD-FORSTER, M.P. 1s. 6d. *Special Edition* on Green Paper for Persons with Weak Eyesight. 2s.
Lessons in Our Laws; or, Talks at Broadacre Farm. By H. F. LESTER, B.A. Parts I. and II., 1s. 6d. each.
Little Folks' History of England. Illustrated. 1s. 6d.
Making of the Home, The. By Mrs. SAMUEL A. BARNETT. 1s. 6d.
Marlborough Books:—Arithmetic Examples, 3s. French Exercises, 3s. 6d. French Grammar, 2s. 6d. German Grammar, 3s. 6d.
Mechanics and Machine Design, Numerical Examples in Practical. By R. G. BLAINE, M.E. *New Edition, Revised and Enlarged.* With 79 Illustrations. Cloth, 2s. 6d.
Mechanics for Young Beginners, A First Book of. By the Rev. J. G. EASTON, M.A. 4s. 6d.

Selections from Cassell & Company's Publications.

Natural History Coloured Wall Sheets Cassell's New. 17 Subjects. Size 39 by 31 in. Mounted on rollers and varnished. 3s. each.

Object Lessons from Nature. By Prof. L. C. MIALL, F.L.S. Fully Illustrated. *New and Enlarged Edition.* Two Vols., 1s. 6d. each.

Physiology for Schools. By A. T. SCHOFIELD, M.D., M.R.C.S., &c. Illustrated. Cloth, 1s. 9d.; Three Parts, paper covers, 5d. each; or cloth limp, 6d. each.

Poetry Readers, Cassell's New. Illustrated. 12 Books, 1d. each; or complete in one Vol., cloth, 1s. 6d.

Popular Educator, Cassell's NEW. With Revised Text, New Maps, New Coloured Plates, New Type, &c. In 8 Vols., 5s. each; or in Four Vols., half-morocco, 50s. the set.

Readers, Cassell's "Belle Sauvage." An entirely New Series. Fully Illustrated. Strongly bound in cloth. (*List on application.*)

Readers, Cassell's "Higher Class." (*List on application.*)

Readers, Cassell's Readable. Illustrated. (*List on application.*)

Readers for Infant Schools, Coloured. Three Books. 4d. each.

Reader, The Citizen. By H. O. ARNOLD-FORSTER, M.P. Illustrated. 1s. 6d. Also a *Scottish Edition*, cloth, 1s. 6d.

Reader, The Temperance. By Rev. J. DENNIS HIRD. 1s. 6d.

Readers, Geographical, Cassell's New. With numerous Illustrations. (*List on application.*)

Readers, The "Modern School" Geographical. (*List on application.*)

Readers, The "Modern School." Illustrated. (*List on application.*)

Reckoning, Howard's Art of. By C. FRUSHER HOWARD. Paper covers, 1s.; cloth, 2s. *New Edition*, 5s.

Round the Empire. By G. R. PARKIN. Fully Illustrated. 1s. 6d.

Science Applied to Work. By J. A. BOWER. 1s.

Science of Everyday Life By J. A. BOWER. Illustrated. 1s.

Shade from Models, Common Objects, and Casts of Ornament, How to. By W. E. SPARKES. With 25 Plates by the Author. 3s.

Shakspere's Plays for School Use. 9 Books. Illustrated. 6d. each.

Spelling, A Complete Manual of. By J. D. MORELL, LL.D. 1s.

Technical Manuals, Cassell's. Illustrated throughout:—
Handrailing and Staircasing, 3s. 6d.—Bricklayers, Drawing for, 3s.—Building Construction, 2s.—Cabinet-Makers, Drawing for, 3s.—Carpenters and Joiners, Drawing for, 3s. 6d.—Gothic Stonework, 3s.—Linear Drawing and Practical Geometry, 2s.—Linear Drawing and Projection. The Two Vols. in One, 3s. 6d.—Machinists and Engineers, Drawing for, 4s. 6d.—Metal-Plate Workers, Drawing for, 3s.—Model Drawing, 3s.—Orthographical and Isometrical Projection, 2s.—Practical Perspective, 3s.—Stonemasons, Drawing for, 3s.—Applied Mechanics, by Sir R. S. Ball, LL.D., 2s.—Systematic Drawing and Shading, 2s.

Technical Educator, Cassell's New. With Coloured Plates and Engravings. Complete in Six Volumes, 5s. each.

Technology, Manuals of. Edited by Prof. AYRTON, F.R.S., and RICHARD WORMELL, D.Sc., M.A. Illustrated throughout:—
The Dyeing of Textile Fabrics, by Prof. Hummel, 5s.—Watch and Clock Making, by D. Glasgow, Vice-President of the British Horological Institute, 4s. 6d.—Steel and Iron, by Prof. W. H. Greenwood, F.C.S., M.I.C.E., &c., 5s.—Spinning Woollen and Worsted, by W. S. B. McLaren, M.P., 4s. 6d.—Design in Textile Fabrics, by T. R. Ashenhurst, 4s. 6d.—Practical Mechanics, by Prof. Perry, M.E., 3s. 6d.—Cutting Tools Worked by Hand and Machine, by Prof. Smith, 3s. 6d.

Things New and Old; or, Stories from English History. By H. O. ARNOLD-FORSTER, M.P. Fully Illustrated, and strongly bound in Cloth. Standards I. & II., 9d. each; Standard III., 1s.; Standard IV., 1s. 3d.; Standards V., VI., & VII., 1s. 6d. each.

This World of Ours. By H. O. ARNOLD-FORSTER, M.P. Illustrated. 3s. 6d.

Selections from Cassell & Company's Publications.

Books for Young People.

"**Little Folks**" **Half-Yearly Volume.** Containing 432 4to pages, with about 200 Illustrations, and Pictures in Colour. Boards, 3s. 6d.; cloth, 5s.

Bo-Peep. A Book for the Little Ones. With Original Stories and Verses. Illustrated throughout. Yearly Volume. Boards, 2s. 6d.; cloth, 3s. 6d.

Beneath the Banner. Being Narratives of Noble Lives and Brave Deeds. By F. J. CROSS. Illustrated, Limp cloth, 1s. Cloth gilt, 2s.

Good Morning! Good Night! By F. J. CROSS. Illustrated. Limp cloth, 1s., or cloth boards, gilt lettered, 2s.

Five Stars in a Little Pool. By EDITH CARRINGTON. Illustrated. 6s.

The Cost of a Mistake. By SARAH PITT. Illustrated. *New Edition.* 2s 6d.

Beyond the Blue Mountains. By L. T. MEADE. 5s.

The Peep of Day. *Cassell's Illustrated Edition.* 2s. 6d.

Maggie Steele's Diary. By E. A. DILLWYN. 2s. 6d.

A Book of Merry Tales. By MAGGIE BROWNE, "SHEILA," ISABEL WILSON, and C. L. MATÉAUX. Illustrated. 3s. 6d.

A Sunday Story-Book. By MAGGIE BROWNE, SAM BROWNE, and AUNT ETHEL. Illustrated. 3s. 6d.

A Bundle of Tales. By MAGGIE BROWNE (Author of "Wanted—a King," &c.), SAM BROWNE, and AUNT ETHEL. 3s. 6d.

Pleasant Work for Busy Fingers. By MAGGIE BROWNE. Illustrated. 5s.

Born a King. By FRANCES and MARY ARNOLD-FORSTER. (The Life of Alfonso XIII., the Boy King of Spain.) Illustrated. 5s.

Cassell's Pictorial Scrap Book. Six Vols. 3s. 6d. each.

Schoolroom and Home Theatricals. By ARTHUR WAUGH. Illustrated. *New Edition.* Paper, 1s. Cloth, 1s. 6d.

Magic at Home. By Prof. HOFFMAN. Illustrated. Cloth gilt, 3s. 6d.

Little Mother Bunch. By Mrs. MOLESWORTH. Illustrated. *New Edition.* Cloth. 2s. 6d.

Heroes of Every-day Life. By LAURA LANE. With about 20 Full-page Illustrations. Cloth. 2s. 6d.

Bob Lovell's Career. By EDWARD S. ELLIS. 5s.

Books for Young People. *Cheap Edition.* Illustrated. Cloth gilt, 3s. 6d. each.

The Champion of Odin; or, Viking Life in the Days of Old. By J. Fred. Hodgetts. | Bound by a Spell; or, The Hunted Witch of the Forest. By the Hon. Mrs. Greene.

Under Bayard's Banner. By Henry Frith.

Books for Young People. Illustrated. 3s. 6d. each.

Told Out of School. By A. J. Daniels.
Red Rose and Tiger Lily. By L. T. Meade.
The Romance of Invention. By James Burnley.
*Baneful Fifteen. By L. T. Meade.
*The White House at Inch Gow. By Mrs. Pitt.
*A Sweet Girl Graduate. By L. T. Meade.
The King's Command: A Story for Girls. By Maggie Symington.

*The Palace Beautiful. By L. T. Meade.
*Polly: A New-Fashioned Girl. By L. T. Meade.
"Follow My Leader." By Talbot Baines Reed.
*A World of Girls: The Story of a School. By L. T. Meade.
Lost among White Africans. By David Ker.
For Fortune and Glory: A Story of the Soudan War. By Lewis Hough.

Also procurable in superior binding, 5s. each.

Selections from Cassell & Company's Publications.

"Peeps Abroad" Library. *Cheap Editions.* Gilt edges, 2s. 6d. each.

Rambles Round London. By C. L. Matéaux. Illustrated.
Around and About Old England. By C. L. Matéaux. Illustrated.
Paws and Claws. By one of the Authors of "Poems written for a Child." Illustrated.
Decisive Events in History. By Thomas Archer. With Original Illustrations.
The True Robinson Crusoes. Cloth gilt.
Peeps Abroad for Folks at Home. Illustrated throughout.
Wild Adventures in Wild Places. By Dr. Gordon Stables, R.N. Illustrated.
Modern Explorers. By Thomas Frost. Illustrated. *New and Cheaper Edition.*
Early Explorers. By Thomas Frost.
Home Chat with our Young Folks. Illustrated throughout.
Jungle, Peak, and Plain. Illustrated throughout.

The "Cross and Crown" Series. Illustrated. 2s. 6d. each.

Freedom's Sword: A Story of the Days of Wallace and Bruce. By Annie S. Swan.
Strong to Suffer: A Story of the Jews. By E. Wynne.
Heroes of the Indian Empire; or, Stories of Valour and Victory. By Ernest Foster.
In Letters of Flame: A Story of the Waldenses. By C. L. Matéaux.
Through Trial to Triumph. By Madeline B. Hunt.
By Fire and Sword: A Story of the Huguenots. By Thomas Archer.
Adam Hepburn's Vow: A Tale of Kirk and Covenant. By Annie S. Swan.
No. XIII.; or, The Story of the Lost Vestal. A Tale of Early Christian Days. By Emma Marshall.

"Golden Mottoes" Series, The. Each Book containing 208 pages, with Four full-page Original Illustrations. Crown 8vo, cloth gilt, 2s. each.

"Nil Desperandum." By the Rev. F. Langbridge, M.A.
"Bear and Forbear." By Sarah Pitt.
"Foremost if I Can." By Helen Atteridge.
"Honour is my Guide." By Jeanie Hering (Mrs. Adams-Acton).
"Aim at a Sure End." By Emily Searchfield.
"He Conquers who Endures." By the Author of "May Cunningham's Trial," &c.

Cassell's Picture Story Books. Each containing about Sixty Pages of Pictures and Stories, &c. 6d. each.

Little Talks.
Bright Stars.
Nursery Toys.
Pet's Posy.
Tiny Tales.
Daisy's Story Book.
Dot's Story Book.
A Nest of Stories.
Good-Night Stories.
Chats for Small Chatterers.
Auntie's Stories.
Birdie's Story Book.
Little Chimes.
A Sheaf of Tales.
Dewdrop Stories.

Illustrated Books for the Little Ones. Containing interesting Stories. All Illustrated. 1s. each; cloth gilt, 1s. 6d.

Bright Tales & Funny Pictures.
Merry Little Tales.
Little Tales for Little People.
Little People and Their Pets.
Tales Told for Sunday.
Sunday Stories for Small People.
Stories and Pictures for Sunday.
Bible Pictures for Boys and Girls.
Firelight Stories.
Sunlight and Shade.
Rub-a-Dub Tales.
Fine Feathers and Fluffy Fur.
Scrambles and Scrapes.
Tittle Tattle Tales.
Up and Down the Garden.
All Sorts of Adventures.
Our Sunday Stories.
Our Holiday Hours.
Indoors and Out.
Some Farm Friends.
Wandering Ways.
Dumb Friends.
Those Golden Sands.
Little Mothers & their Children.
Our Pretty Pets.
Our Schoolday Hours.
Creatures Tame.
Creatures Wild.

Selections from Cassell & Company's Publications.

Cassell's Shilling Story Books. All Illustrated, and containing Interesting Stories.

Bunty and the Boys.
The Heir of Elmdale.
The Mystery at Shoncliff School.
Claimed at Last, & Roy's Reward.
Thorns and Tangles.
The Cuckoo in the Robin's Nest.
John's Mistake. [Pitchers.
The History of Five Little Diamonds in the Sand.
Surly Bob.
The Giant's Cradle.
Shag and Doll.
Aunt Lucia's Locket.
The Magic Mirror.
The Cost of Revenge.
Clever Frank.
Among the Redskins.
The Ferryman of Brill.
Harry Maxwell.
A Banished Monarch.
Seventeen Cats.

"Wanted—a King" Series. *Cheap Edition.* Illustrated. 2s. 6d. each.

Great Grandmemma. By Georgina M. Synge.
Robin's Ride. By Ellinor Davenport Adams.
Wanted—a King; or, How Merle set the Nursery Rhymes to Rights. By Maggie Browne. With Original Designs by Harry Furniss.
Fairy Tales in Other Lands. By Julia Goddard.

The World's Workers. A Series of New and Original Volumes. With Portraits printed on a tint as Frontispiece. 1s. each.

John Cassell. By G. Holden Pike.
Charles Haddon Spurgeon. By G. Holden Pike.
Dr. Arnold of Rugby. By Rose E. Selfe.
The Earl of Shaftesbury. By Henry Frith.
Sarah Robinson, Agnes Weston, and Mrs. Meredith. By E. M. Tomkinson.
Thomas A. Edison and Samuel F. B. Morse. By Dr. Denslow and J. Marsh Parker.
Mrs. Somerville and Mary Carpenter. By Phyllis Browne.
General Gordon. By the Rev. S. A. Swaine.
Charles Dickens. By his Eldest Daughter.
Sir Titus Salt and George Moore. By J. Burnley.
Florence Nightingale, Catherine Marsh, Frances Ridley Havergal, Mrs. Ranyard ("L. N. R."). By Lizzie Alldridge.
Dr. Guthrie, Father Mathew, Elihu Burritt, George Livesey. By John W. Kirton, LL.D.
Sir Henry Havelock and Colin Campbell Lord Clyde. By E. C. Phillips.
Abraham Lincoln. By Ernest Foster.
George Müller and Andrew Reed. By E. R. Pitman.
Richard Cobden. By R. Cowing.
Benjamin Franklin. By E. M. Tomkinson.
Handel. By Eliza Clarke. [Swaine.
Turner the Artist. By the Rev. S. A.
George and Robert Stephenson. By C. L. Matéaux.
David Livingstone. By Robert Smiles.

*** *The above Works can also be had Three in One Vol., cloth, gilt edges, 3s.*

Library of Wonders. Illustrated Gift-books for Boys. Paper, 1s.; cloth, 1s. 6d.

Wonderful Balloon Ascents.
Wonderful Adventures.
Wonderful Escapes.
Wonders of Animal Instinct.
Wonders of Bodily Strength and Skill.

Cassell's Eighteenpenny Story Books. Illustrated.

Wee Willie Winkie.
Ups and Downs of a Donkey's Life.
Three Wee Ulster Lassies.
Up the Ladder.
Dick's Hero; and other Stories.
The Chip Boy.
Raggles, Baggles, and the Emperor.
Roses from Thorns.
Faith's Father.
By Land and Sea.
The Young Berringtons.
Jeff and Leff.
Tom Morris's Error.
Worth more than Gold.
"Through Flood—Through Fire;" and other Stories.
The Girl with the Golden Locks.
Stories of the Olden Time.

Gift Books for Young People. By Popular Authors. With Four Original Illustrations in each. Cloth gilt, 1s. 6d. each.

The Boy Hunters of Kentucky. By Edward S. Ellis.
Red Feather: a Tale of the American Frontier. By Edward S. Ellis.
Seeking a City.
Rhoda's Reward; or, "If Wishes were Horses."
Jack Marston's Anchor.
Frank's Life-Battle; or, The Three Friends.
Fritters. By Sarah Pitt.
The Two Hardcastles. By Madeline Bonavia Hunt.
Major Monk's Motto. By the Rev. F. Langbridge.
Trixy. By Maggie Symington.
Rags and Rainbows: A Story of Thanksgiving.
Uncle William's Charges; or, The Broken Trust.
Pretty Pink's Purpose; or, The Little Street Merchants.
Tim Thomson's Trial. By George Weatherly.
Ursula's Stumbling-Block. By Julia Goddard.
Ruth's Life-Work. By the Rev. Joseph Johnson.

Selections from Cassell & Company's Publications.

Cassell's Two-Shilling Story Books. Illustrated.

- Margaret's Enemy.
- Stories of the Tower.
- Mr. Burke's Nieces.
- May Cunningham's Trial.
- The Top of the Ladder: How to Reach it.
- Little Flotsam.
- Madge and Her Friends.
- The Children of the Court.
- Maid Marjory.
- Peggy, and other Tales.
- The Four Cats of the Tippertons.
- Marion's Two Homes.
- Little Folks' Sunday Book.
- Two Fourpenny Bits.
- Poor Nelly.
- Tom Heriot.
- Through Peril to Fortune.
- Aunt Tabitha's Waifs.
- In Mischief Again.

Cheap Editions of Popular Volumes for Young People. Bound in cloth, gilt edges, 2s. 6d. each.

- In Quest of Gold; or, Under the Whanga Falls.
- On Board the *Esmeralda*; or, Martin Leigh's Log.
- For Queen and King.
- Esther West.
- Three Homes.
- Working to Win.
- Perils Afloat and Brigands Ashore.

Books by Edward S. Ellis. Illustrated. Cloth, 2s. 6d. each.

- The Great Cattle Trail.
- The Path in the Ravine.
- The Young Ranchers.
- The Hunters of the Ozark.
- The Camp in the Mountains.
- Ned in the Woods. A Tale of Early Days in the West.
- Down the Mississippi.
- The Last War Trail.
- Ned on the River. A Tale of Indian River Warfare.
- Footprints in the Forest.
- Up the Tapajos.
- Ned in the Block House. A Story of Pioneer Life in Kentucky.
- The Lost Trail.
- Camp-Fire and Wigwam.
- Lost in the Wilds.
- Lost in Samoa. A Tale of Adventure in the Navigator Islands.
- Tad; or, "Getting Even" with Him.

The "World in Pictures." Illustrated throughout. *Cheap Edition.* 1s. 6d. each.

- A Ramble Round France.
- All the Russias.
- Chats about Germany.
- The Eastern Wonderland (Japan).
- Glimpses of South America.
- Round Africa.
- The Land of Temples (India).
- The Isles of the Pacific.
- Peeps into China
- The Land of Pyramids (Egypt).

Half-Crown Story Books.

- Pictures of School Life and Boyhood.
- Pen's Perplexities.
- At the South Pole.

Books for the Little Ones.

- Rhymes for the Young Folk. By William Allingham. Beautifully Illustrated. 3s. 6d.
- The History Scrap Book; With nearly 1,000 Engravings. Cloth, 7s. 6d.
- The Sunday Scrap Book. With Several Hundred Illustrations. Paper boards, 3s. 6d.; cloth, gilt edges, 5s.
- The Old Fairy Tales. With Original Illustrations. Boards, 1s.; cloth, 1s. 6d.

Albums for Children. 3s. 6d. each.

- The Album for Home, School, and Play. Containing Stories by Popular Authors. Illustrated.
- My Own Album of Animals. With Full-page Illustrations.
- Picture Album of All Sorts. With Full-page Illustrations.
- The Chit-Chat Album. Illustrated throughout.

Cassell & Company's Complete Catalogue *will be sent post free on application to*

CASSELL & COMPANY, LIMITED, *Ludgate Hill, London.*

www.ingramcontent.com/pod-product-compliance
Lightning Source LLC
Chambersburg PA
CBHW021829230426
43669CB00008B/910